THE BEAUTIFUL GAME
how to master football *and* your own life

JASON TILLETT

ABOUT THE AUTHOR

Jason Tillett is a PhD student in philosophy at the University of Queensland. His thesis is on Spinoza's conception of human freedom. He has a Master of Philosophy from the University of Adelaide. He also has a First Class Honours degree, for which he was awarded the University Medal, and a Bachelor of Laws from Flinders University.

Tillett grew up in Davoren Park, a suburb in South Australia known for its high unemployment and crime rates. He was constantly in trouble with the police and was expelled from almost every school he attended. Eventually, no secondary school in South Australia would accept him. Tillett smoked cigarettes and took a variety of drugs from about the age of ten until he was twenty-four. He regularly experienced and witnessed acts of violence during this period of his life. His friends were violent offenders, drug dealers, armed robbers and thieves. Nearly everyone Tillett knew was unemployed, in and out of prison, had been killed or had taken their own life. Education rescued him from a similar fate.

The author lives in South Australia with his wife and son.

Published by Jason Tillett

Copyright © 2018. All rights reserved. No portion of this publication may be used, reproduced or transmitted by any means, digital, electronic, mechanical, photocopy or recording without written permission of the publisher, except in the case of brief quotations within critical articles or reviews.

ISBN: 978-0-6483256-0-4 (paperback)

First edition, 2018

For book orders and enquiries, contact:
Jason Tillett
email: jttbg2018@gmail.com

For Aiting and Alexander, my wife and son

ACKNOWLEDGEMENTS

I would like to thank Howard Jillings, Eddie Eyers, Adam Allison, Bevin Wilson and Aiting Zhu for reading an early draft of the book. Their comments, feedback and encouragement helped me to improve the book and bring it to fruition. I also want to thank Judith Nickels for proofreading the book and Hardshell Publishing for designing the cover, formatting the book and typesetting the text.

AUTHOR'S NOTE

This book is a source of principles and ideas that can help you to improve your abilities or overcome challenges in football or life. The relevance and utility of the ideas and principles will depend on the reader's personal circumstances. For this reason, the word 'you' and its counterparts are used in the general sense. It is up to the reader to decide what is in the book that is useful or valuable for them. The principles and ideas in the book will be new to many readers, but I hope that even people who have played the games of football or life for a long time will discover novel insights or at least an alternative way of thinking about football or life. The book introduces philosophical ideas and important thinkers in the hope that they will inspire the reader to explore them further.

CONTENTS

Introduction xi

Part One: The World Game 1
    1. Football and life are games we play 3
    2. Causality is woven into the fabric of the universe 7
    3. The realisation of our dreams is at the mercy of the stars 12
    4. The most successful are the luckiest 16
    5. Truth and reality exist 20

Part Two: Ethics 23
    6. With rules, harmony; without rules, disharmony 25
    7. A rule has force only if its violation is noticed 29
    8. For there to be a winner, there must be a loser 32
    9. The jersey has the power to unite and to divide 34
    10. The good of the individual depends on the good of the team ... 40
    11. The 'unsung heroes' are just as valuable as the superstars 43
    12. Ability compels respect 46

Part Three: Desire, Love and Passion 49
    13. Whoever wants the ball most is most likely to get it 51
    14. Passion gives purpose and purpose gives life meaning 54

15. Motivation is initiated and sustained by external things 57
  16. The human ego is a charming serpent 62
  17. We imitate powerful people... 67

Part Four: Practical Wisdom 71
  18. Knowledge is power 73
  19. All human creations and achievements can be traced to ideas ... 79
  20. Understanding enables us to appreciate the game 83
  21. The more you can do and the better you understand
      the game, the more you will enjoy it 88
  22. A wise player looks up 91
  23. Communication is the most fundamental human skill 94
  24. Simplicity is superior to complexity 97
  25. Rushing invites error 100
  26. Even the best players miss more than they score 103
  27. Courage is focusing on doing what you must 106
  28. Only you are within your power 109
  29. Preparation tames anxiety... 113
  30. People tend to forget their origins 119
  31. The game will not stop for you 123
  32. Suffering is a natural part of the game 126
  33. The journey makes the greatest joy possible 130
  34. It is up to you to decide to appreciate a moment 133
  35. Self-mastery is the highest good 136

Part Five: The Beautiful Game 141
  36. Beauty expresses excellence 143
  37. Creativity is unoriginal 145
  38. Without the ordinary, there can be no extraordinary 148
  39. Resolution conquers adversity 151

Conclusion 155

INTRODUCTION

FOOTBALL—SOCCER—IS just a game, right? To non-football fans, this might be obvious. But, fans know football is more than just a game. It is a religion. It is life. Football is so important that it can provoke tears in both the winners and losers of a World Cup final. Victory in a football match can make a whole nation jubilant, whereas defeat can send a whole nation into a fit of depression.

To many people, this kind of behaviour seems ridiculous. It may be hard to understand why some people follow their team so devotedly and passionately. Fans cheer, jeer and cry depending on what befalls their beloved footballing heroes. They may even hate the opposition and their opponents' fans. All this nonsense perplexes the non-football fan.

What if football is a microcosm of life? What if all you see in football, the things you think are silly, crazy or don't understand, are part of everyday life? That you are playing a game while reading the words on this page? That the principles, rules, experiences and lessons that apply in football operate in your own life? We don't need to wonder about these 'what if' questions because I am here to show that, like football, life is a game and that the principles that govern the game of football also govern the game of life.

Imagine you were thrown into the game of football without ever having heard of the game or seen it played. You would be completely ignorant of the rules, skills, knowledge and philosophy that govern and organise the game and your participation in it. What would you do? The short answer is that you wouldn't know what to do. And, yet, everyone has experienced this type of situation, for every human being that has ever existed has been thrown into the game of life.

We do not enter the world with insight into the nature of life, its rules, and its principles. We are born helpless, feeble and ignorant. We rely on fellow human beings not only for survival, but also for our chances of being successful in life, for the people in our environment, such as our parents, siblings, friends and teachers are our sources of information about the game of life. In the earliest years of our lives, we rely on other people for information about what the game is, how it came to be, how it works, what its rules are, and the ideas and skills needed to play it well. As we get older, we continue to seek information from people who are older, wiser or more experienced than us about a particular area of life, like work or relationships, so that we can make the best decisions.

Suppose your coach misinformed you about how the game of football works and provided you with bad strategies. What would your performance be like? Similarly, consider the possibility that the people in your life were wrong or provided you with inaccurate information. I'm not suggesting that the important people in your life have misguided you. It is likely you acquired at least some good advice. It varies from person to person.

On the other hand, how many of us really try to understand the principles of life and actively strive to apply them to our own lives? In my experience, a tiny percentage of people do so. This is either because they don't care, they are sceptics, they are obstructed by other people or life circumstances, or worse, they think they already know, which is usually contradicted by their complaints and bad results. The greatest obstacle to understanding is thinking we already know fully that which we do not know. For this reason, we must remember to keep our minds open when we seek to understand new ideas.

Just as we need guidance from the best coaches to fulfil our potential as footballers, we need to learn insights from the masters of life so that we can thrive in it. The people who can teach us about the game of life could be people we know with a lot of life experience, wise people on television or people online who have succeeded in certain areas of their lives and impart the lessons they have learned. Alternatively, we can acquire wisdom from books written by people who have discovered the secrets to success in life. Another way is to reflect on our own life experiences.

My comparison of the good football coach to people wise in the game of life is the type of thinking that inspired my idea for this book. To be able to understand principles derived from analogies and how an idea in one area—football—applies in another—life in general—is the kind of thinking that can enhance our ability to think for ourselves and understand how things work. A highly developed power to think analogically, which is a form of reflective thinking, empowers us to think for ourselves. The more we can think for ourselves, the greater our self-trust. With self-trust comes personal power and self-confidence.

This book, then, is an exercise in analogical and reflective thinking. By reading the analogies between football and life covered in this book, not only will you discover ideas that can help you improve your game as a footballer or as a life player, you will also develop your ability to think analogically and reflectively. As the ancient Greek philosopher Aristotle said, we become what we habitually do. By repeatedly thinking analogically and reflectively about football and life, this habit will become part of your mind, which you can then apply to every other part of your life and any subject you are interested in.

Throughout the book there are references to philosophers, scientists and other wise people. Their insights help to explain or express the ideas and principles in the book. Multiple references are made to Ralph Waldo Emerson, the 19th century American philosopher, essayist and poet, because of his eloquence and insight into human nature. The philosophy of Benedict de Spinoza, the 17th century Dutch philosopher, has much to teach us about life and the nature of human emotions. Spinoza's philosophy was the subject of my Master's thesis and is central to my PhD thesis. The renowned neuroscientist Antonio Damasio shows that Spinoza anticipated the contemporary neuroscientific view of human emotions. This makes Spinoza's ideas particularly useful. Incorporation of the ideas of philosophers into my analysis of football and life may result in a deeper and more interesting presentation.

You might wonder why I chose to focus on football instead of some other sport. Football involves and expresses human nature in myriad ways (as we will see later) and, after all, it is called 'the world game'. So, for me, it makes sense to focus on football rather than another sport. Of course, many of the ideas in this book apply to other sports, and reflection on other sports can lead to interesting insights that are applicable to life, as well as football and yet other sports. All insights from reflection on football, other sports and life are valuable, since they contribute to improving our ability to think for ourselves and to understand and play the game of life as well as possible.

I believe that application of the principles in this book to your own life will help you to overcome personal problems and increase your chances of success in football or life. I believe this because I have applied these principles to my own life and my participation in football, and I have consequently achieved positive results. However, I should make it clear that I am not a professional footballer.

Except for a short period when I was about eight years old, I didn't play football properly and regularly until the age of eighteen. Even though I was too old to begin the journey to become a professional footballer, I wanted to play football socially. I had not really tried to learn how to play football until this age. Therefore, my skills and understanding of the game were mediocre. Nevertheless, I managed to change myself from a footballer with zero confidence and skill to a confident player who could use his skills with the ball in social games.

My early childhood and teenage years were a disaster. I grew up in Davoren Park, one of the most disadvantaged suburbs in Australia. I was expelled from nearly every school I attended, including a 'last chance school' I was forced to attend because of my problematic behaviour. Before the age of sixteen I had exhausted my mainstream educational opportunities. Now, I'm a graduate of law. I was awarded a First Class Honours degree and a University Medal. I have a Master's degree and I am in the final year of a PhD in philosophy.

Changing one's own life can be extremely difficult. For example, before I succeeded I repeatedly failed to stop taking drugs and smoking cigarettes. Most people from disadvantaged areas like Davoren Park know how hard it is to change and to escape an undesirable life. Here are two anecdotes to illustrate the scepticism I encountered when I expressed my desire to live a better life.

In my mid-teens, I said to a 'good' friend that I was going to study law one day. He laughed in my face and said I had no chance of that happening. My friend was with me on the day I was awarded a Bachelor of Laws degree.

In my second year of university, I regularly travelled to Davoren Park to visit my mother. I got off the train at the Elizabeth station. A guy I used to hang out with in my teens was there. He was pleased to see me. He said, 'You still studying law?' I replied, 'Yeah.' My friend said, 'Yeah, I'm still doing armed robberies.'

My second friend's comment indicates the kind of background I come from. It also illustrates the doubt my friend had about me escaping the disadvantage we had both experienced throughout our young lives. Many people were sceptical about my ambition to study law and my desire to give up smoking cigarettes and taking drugs. Even though my family and friends were initially doubtful (and some of them unsupportive), most congratulated me on achieving these goals. This taught me that you must believe in and rely on yourself; when few or no people believe in you or there is little support available.

Only when your desire to change or improve yourself is stronger than your other habits or desires will you do so. Once you strongly desire to improve yourself, you then need good ideas and principles to guide your decision-making. My transformation, in football and my personal life, is due to my *applying* the principles I learned, or derived from my reflections on football and my life experiences. By developing the ability to reflect on your life and actions and learning how to see the relationship between things, you too can improve your ability to think for yourself, make better decisions and become a better footballer or player in the game of life.

Within the pages of this book you will discover thirty-nine principles that govern the games of football and life. Each chapter discusses a principle. The principle is expressed in the title of the chapter, for example, 'Preparation tames anxiety'. A principle can be expressed in words in various ways, but the principle itself is unalterable, for it is a fundamental truth or law. The body of the chapter explains and illustrates the principle, and then suggests how it can be applied in our own lives. The principles can be applied individually, but, as one would expect, their interconnectedness suggests that they are most effective when they are used with other related principles.

This book is written from the perspective of a football fan, a philosopher and a realist. I've played football intermittently for about twenty years. During this time, I've been a passionate fan of 'the beautiful game'. I love to play and to watch the game played by the best. As a philosopher, I am constantly reflecting on my life, thinking and activities. Even though the ideas in this book might be controversial, I know they are applicable to real life because they have worked for me. The ideas in this book can help you conquer your problems, fulfil your potential as a footballer or a human being and to live a good life.

Football is known as the world game because people from nearly every country in the world play and love the game. Life is a world game, too, since everyone in the world *must* play the game of life. The highest aim of both games is to play them beautifully.

PART ONE

THE WORLD GAME

THE FIFA WORLD Cup is the second biggest sporting event, behind the Olympics. This is astonishing given that the Olympics involves numerous sports, including football. For many people around the world, football is a religion and its greatest players are worshipped as gods. The hope of witnessing a divine act in a football match on the world stage is what makes us tune in.

Part One provides a 'big picture' view of football and life. By providing a big picture view, we can better understand the other parts of the game, such as ethics and what we should do to flourish in football or life. This part begins with an exploration of the nature of a game and explains why both football and life are games. The law of cause and effect, the role of luck, and the relation between reality and its interpretation are among the ideas discussed in this part because they are fundamental to the games of football and life.

1

FOOTBALL AND LIFE ARE GAMES WE PLAY

FOOTBALL IS A game. In general, a game involves a goal, rules, equipment, competitors, a winner and a loser, skills and a referee. All fans know that the main aim of football is to score more goals than your opponent. A related rule is that a goal will be awarded only when the whole ball crosses the goal line. You are not allowed to punch the ball over the goal line, like the magician Diego Maradona did. His goal counted though, because the whole ball crossed the line and the referee did not see his handball.

Examples of football equipment are boots, a ball and goalkeeper gloves. There are two sides competing against each other. The skills needed to play the game include the ability to dribble, pass and strike the ball, which are required to score goals and win a match. There is also the referee who enforces the rules. The above components structure and regulate the game.

To be permitted to play in a game of football—one in which all involved want real competition—you must know and play by the rules. To achieve success, you must know the written, or explicit, rules and the unwritten ones. If you do not know strategy, those who do will run circles around you. You also need to know and practice football skills. They are essential to competence in the game.

Life is a game. Some people deny this. They might say that life is a sacred experience, a journey in a mysterious world, or perhaps some kind of test. I don't disagree with these descriptions of life. It can be described in those ways, but it is also a game.

Many years ago, I said to a friend that life is a game. She denied it. I asked her to identify something in life that she thought was not a game. Her answer was 'conversation'. Here is the response I gave to my friend: 'Conversation has a goal. The *goal* is to communicate information; for example, our ideas, feelings and desires. There are *rules* of conversation. We should be polite, listen and not talk over the top of the other person. We have *equipment*, such as our vocabulary, body language, our tone of voice, and our ideas.'

Now, I concede that conversation is not obviously a competition in the same way as football. Empathetic communicators cooperate with each other. They listen to what people say, read their body language and give considered responses. However, I'm sure most of us have had conversations that very much seemed like competitions. There is a sense in which many people compete to kick the goal of communication via their thoughts and feelings. Some people dominate the conversation and others say little or nothing. One is kicking goals, while the other is conceding goals.

Most of us are familiar with the observation that often people are not really listening, rather are preparing what they want to say. They want to be heard more than they want to hear the other person's viewpoint. That is a kind of competition. There is a winner in the sense that whoever has their voice heard, and whoever expresses their thoughts and feelings most is the winner. The person who is ignored is the loser.

There are *skills* in conversation too: choosing your words carefully, using body language to express your intentions and feelings, judging correctly when to speak and when to listen and so on. There is a *referee*, represented by other people or it can be your own conscience. If you are rude or disrespectful, others will pull you up. If your views are extreme or offensive, you are likely to get a straight red. Your time in the game of conversation is over.

We must understand that conversation is a game and we need to know the rules and skills of the game if we want to play it well. The same applies to other areas of life.

The idea that life is a game is distasteful to many of us. But, just because it is distasteful does not mean it's untrue. If you think life is something higher than a game, I suspect you are one of those people who wonder why human beings are rude or arrogant, and lust after power and fame. Only people ignorant of human nature think this way.

The principles of nature and human nature are the rules of the game of life. The goal of the game of life is to maximise your wellbeing. Your wellbeing consists in your natural power by which you strive to preserve and increase your power (this idea is covered in chapters 16, 20 and 32). All things in nature are competing to achieve this goal. If you learn these principles and accept life is a game, you will not wonder why people behave in the ways described above. And nothing prevents us from simultaneously accepting life is a game and that human dignity is important.

Ignorance of the laws of nature and human nature makes us vulnerable to the world outside us. The wise approach to life, then, is to acquire knowledge of these laws. People from a wide range of backgrounds have discovered the principles of life. However, one need not be a recognised scientist or philosopher to know the principles or laws, for reflection on human experience often leads to their discovery. There are likely to be people you know who have played the game of life for a long time, reflected on it and learned valuable lessons. You can improve yourself as a life player by learning the principles of life from these people.

If we want to play the game of life well, we must learn the rules and skills of the game and do our best. To this end, it is important that we understand life is a game.

2

CAUSALITY IS WOVEN INTO THE FABRIC OF THE UNIVERSE

THE UNIVERSE IS governed by the law of cause and effect. For every given cause, there is an effect that must follow it. This is a controversial claim. The heads of many physicists and philosophers would have burst upon reading it, for they think 'the uncertainty principle' contradicts this law of nature. But, even *if* there are parts of the universe that defy the law of cause and effect, a hypothesis I doubt (as did Albert Einstein, other physicists and philosophers), human actions and experiences confirm the existence of this law. When you kick the ball (cause), the ball moves in a certain direction (effect). When you make the ball cross your opponents' goal line (cause), the referee awards your team a goal (effect). We could generate countless examples. This just shows that football is part of the universe and that it is also governed by the law of cause and effect.

The aim of football is to put the ball in the back of the net. Usually, there must be several passes and then a shot on goal. Each pass or shot is a cause. The effect is the way the ball leaves a player's boot and reaches the next player. A pass that falls short is one of the causes of the next play, created by the player who made the pass. The effect of the ball falling short is that the teammate must work harder to try to retain possession. This makes it difficult for the player to keep the ball and get it to another player on their team.

The converse is true, too. If the pass is good, the next player will find it easier to keep possession of the ball. For every positive cause, for example, for every good pass, you are more likely to produce the effect you are after, for example, a completed pass, and finally, to help score a goal.

Your foot moving the ball is only one of many causes in the game of football. There are physical and mental causes. The physical causes include things like your technique, how much power you apply to the ball, body strength, positioning on the pitch, timing of your run, your field of vision, the turf and noise of the crowd. The mental causes include things like judgement, level of confidence, strength of desire, how you feel, what you believe, prejudices, self-concept and memory.

Each person on the football pitch (twenty-two players, the referee and assistants) is composed of both physical and mental causes. These causes combine to produce the effects that make up a football match. It is often hard to predict the outcome of a match, for the outcome (an effect) is determined by innumerable causes that are unforeseeable and imperceptible.

It is important to recognise that when you play the game of football, you are part of a causal system. You are a cause made up of many causes that affect the events of the game. You can be a positive or a negative cause. Learn to be a positive cause, that is, a footballer who produces good effects like accurate passes and well-timed runs. You should also learn to read the causes and effects of the game. If you can identify the causes, you can influence or even control the effects.

You are a cause and an effect in the game of life. You are the effect of the actions of your parents; for example, your mother gave birth to you. Your passion for football may be the effect of your parents taking you to football matches. You are the cause to some extent of what other people think, feel, say or do. If you ask a friend what they have been up to, this causes them to think of what they have been doing. If you yell at your children or your parents, you in part cause them to feel sad or angry. If you ask someone a question or for something from them, you, in part, cause their response. For example, you determine the subject matter of their thought and speech. And, if you ask someone to do something for you and they want to do it, you partly cause them to do it for you.

Many of us are unaware of our causal power and influence over ourselves and others. This lack of awareness can be dangerous because it means this power and influence is exercised or expressed blindly to a large extent. If you do not choose your words carefully, you could make another person hate you when what you wanted to do was help them.

Let's say someone you care about behaves inappropriately. A blind approach would be to call them a 'trouble-maker'. For many reasons, the person will feel upset and unjustly treated by this, mainly because it is an absolute statement that ignores other attributes they possess, many of them positive. It is better to identify the action, say, using your car without your permission, highlighting the potentially dangerous consequences of what they did and explaining that you do not want them or anyone else to be harmed.

This can be applied to yourself. Maybe you got a low test score. You tell yourself that you are not smart enough to do x, perhaps to be a doctor or lawyer. This self-talk is likely to result in low self-esteem, associated with your view of your abilities. On another test you probably will not try as hard as you could because you will judge it a waste of time, since you do not consider yourself smart enough to be whatever it is you want to be. If you instead think, 'I did not spend enough time learning about subject x, which is why I did not answer the question correctly', you will feel more hopeful because you have interpreted it as a problem that you have the power to fix. This is the opposite of identifying a bad result with your whole self, whereby you believe it follows from an unchangeable you.

Recognise that everything you say and do to yourself and others has causal power. Even though your words and actions may contribute little to the effect, it behoves you to use that power wisely. You need to become clear about why you are saying or doing what you are saying or doing. That way, you can figure out what words and actions would be most effective.

Family is an area of life that requires prudent use of causal power. Ideally, your family would function like a sequence of passes executed flawlessly by FC Barcelona. However, it might be up to you to be the initial positive cause that sets up your family to work together to make each member happy. Perhaps your relationship with a family member could be improved by substituting a negative attitude for a positive one. For example, rather than criticise, encourage; rather than label, identify and explain.

Unfortunately, some of us are stuck on a team of ignorant, selfish and unskilled teammates, be they family members, friends, colleagues or acquaintances. Perhaps what you do has little power to produce the effect of victory. You could allow yourself to imitate the rest of your team and compound the suffering. Regardless of your situation, you are a cause and you could be a positive cause, which, if applied, must produce commensurate effects.

Undoubtedly, our positive actions can be counterbalanced or overpowered by the negative actions of other people. Still, the composite effect (that is, the overall impact of the words and actions of everyone involved) depends on the *strength* of its contributing causes. Positive causes (in the form of your words and actions) must produce positive effects that express their power. So, your attempts to assist *must* influence your teammates to some extent.

Some of us can leave dysfunctional teams. For those of us who lack this option, we must be content with the knowledge that we can be positive or negative causes. Just as you can do your best to ensure the ball arrives at the feet of your teammate, you can ensure that your words and actions assist the people you are close to in your personal, social or professional lives.

3

THE REALISATION OF OUR DREAMS IS AT THE MERCY OF THE STARS

WE ALL ENJOY the special moments in a football match. We want to score the goal that wins the game or make a game-saving tackle. What we often fail to realise is that many causes beyond our own control must work in our favour for us to get the chance to create that special moment. A match in the 2013 FIFA Confederations Cup demonstrates this principle. The match was Brazil versus Italy.

At the start of the game, no one could have predicted that a dream moment was in store for one of the players. Prior to this momentous event, the game had been uninspiring. A player who started on the bench changed the game. Dante, soon after entering the game, scored a goal for his country, Brazil. He was born and raised in Salvador, the place where the match was being played, which made it a special moment for him, his teammates and the local fans.

No one could have foreseen the line of dominos that needed to topple for Dante's special moment to eventuate. David Luiz was clearly the first choice in Dante's position of central defender. Luiz likely would have played the whole game if he was not injured or sent off. Luiz hurt his leg after he tackled the Italian player Candreva. He appeared to shake it off and was okay. But, in the thirty-second minute, Luiz dropped to the ground. The injury was bad. He needed to be substituted.

In came Dante, the local boy. The home fans cheered for Dante as he walked onto the pitch. It was his first appearance in the Confederations Cup. Just before the end of the first half, Neymar won a free kick outside the 18-yard box. He then whipped the ball into the goal area. Fred headed the ball straight at the goalkeeper Gianluigi Buffon, who palmed the ball directly to Dante. Dante, who received the ball inside the 6-yard box, guided the ball into the back of the net. The local boy had scored his first international goal for Brazil in front of his home supporters. The crowd erupted with passionate delight, his teammates, who knew he was from Salvador, were overjoyed and enthusiastically celebrated his special moment with him.

Consider the causes outside Dante's control that led to the opportunity to score the goal. Luiz needed to be injured. It was up to the coach, Luiz Felipe Scolari, to select Dante to replace Luiz. Neymar had to win the free kick. Fred had to head the ball at the goal and Buffon push it directly to Dante. Buffon might have pushed the ball somewhere else. There was no defender in front of Dante who could have obstructed his shot on goal. He was in the right place, at the right time. All those causes were beyond his control. The goal was a gift of fortune.

Obviously, Dante had to put himself in the position to take the opportunity to score the goal. He was on the national team of Brazil. That means he had worked hard and had considerable ability as a footballer. His skill and composure, the products of hard work and training, enabled him to take his chance and make the dream moment materialise. As the adage goes, *success is when preparation meets opportunity.*

It is worthwhile highlighting the things that are beyond our control, for human beings usually focus on individuals and achievements, which might give the impression that their successes are the result of their own efforts *alone*. For instance, on the highlights program you might simply see that Dante scored a goal and think he is a good player because of that fact. The problem is that the highlight leaves out the causal story, which provides perspective.

This perspective can help us ensure that our expectations of ourselves and others are realistic. We might see someone score goals and try to emulate them only to be frustrated. The best players have gone long spells without scoring goals, for example Ronaldo (the Brazilian), Cristiano Ronaldo, Lionel Messi, Fernando Torres, Eden Hazard and many other top attacking players. We need to acknowledge the forces beyond our own powers and the immense role luck plays in individual moments of brilliance and the great successes of a football team.

This principle applies to life. Barack Obama was the first black president of the United States. He could not have been the president a century ago. The external circumstances—racism and the oppression of black people in the United States—made it impossible for any black person to be president at that time. This shows that we need to be aware of the things that are within our power and acknowledge that the realisation of a dream involves a large slice of luck, be it in the form of social or personal circumstances.

In my first year of university (at the age of twenty-five), life bestowed serendipity upon me. On a whim, I decided to enter a shop to get some change for the university printing machine. In the shop was a family friend who I had not seen since I was nine years old. After our meeting, I lived with the family friend for several years in a middle-class suburb, having come from an impoverished and disadvantaged area. Instead of living in a house with heroin addicts as neighbours, my neighbours were doctors, a successful car businessman and a retired engineer with whom I spoke on a couple of occasions. The family friend is one of the wisest and kindest people I have ever known. He shared his wisdom with me and inspired me to focus on ethics in my philosophy studies. I did not manufacture this blessing; the stars aligned for me.

Many of the best moments in life have little to do with our abilities and efforts and more to do with good fortune.

4

THE MOST SUCCESSFUL ARE THE LUCKIEST

THE DIFFERENCE BETWEEN principle 3 and this principle is that the former highlights causes outside our control and the latter emphasises the misapprehension of the nature of success. We are told by authority figures, be they educators, professional athletes or business people, that success is the result of diligence guided by intelligence. The most successful people in football or other areas of life attribute their success chiefly to hard work, even though they will often give some credit to inborn talent. So, most of us are likely to deny that the most successful people in life are the luckiest.

David Beckham, Zinedine Zidane and Cristiano Ronaldo are great players that worked very hard to perfect their skills. It seems that their skills, which are the result of their own efforts, are responsible for their success. It would be foolish to deny that skill or ability, and the hard work needed to produce them, have no role in defending, passing or shooting the ball well. Obviously, without technique or skill it's extremely difficult to beat a world-class goalkeeper. Skill or ability, and hard work, are certainly needed to score goals or win a trophy.

The first thing to do is to explain what luck is and then to contrast it with achieving something, like scoring a goal, through our own efforts alone. Luck, another name for fortune, is some good thing or outcome that cannot be attributed solely to our efforts and abilities. As Spinoza says, 'the gifts of fortune [are] matters which are not in our power'.

Say you want to kick the ball into the back of the net on the right side of the goal, without a goalkeeper defending the goal line. Suppose you have practiced doing this for a long time and concentrate and execute your skill well. When the ball brushes the right post as it goes into the back of the net, we can say that it was not luck, but your skill and ability that resulted in you scoring the goal.

Now, imagine you had to get the ball past a world-class goalkeeper like Manuel Neuer or Gianluigi Buffon. Whether you score the goal depends not only on the goalkeeper guessing where you will kick the ball, their agility and the strength in their hands, things that are beyond your control, but also how you feel, for example, your confidence and anxiety levels. Even if it is more likely you will score the penalty than miss it, the attributes of the goalkeeper and your feelings, like anxiety, which you cannot really control, contribute to the outcome. In other words, you are lucky if you score a goal from a penalty kick against Neuer or Buffon.

Consider what happens when all the players on the football pitch have roughly the same skill level. Messi would effortlessly dribble the ball past a bunch of amateurs, but it is not so easy to beat elite defenders and goalkeepers. That is why Messi does not score a goal every time he touches the ball. What I have found when I have watched the elite players (and even the goals I've seen and scored in very modest competitions), is that most goals and beautiful moves occur when a player, his teammates and the ball are in the right place at the right time.

While reflecting on this principle and watching football matches, I became aware that virtually all the goals scored were ultimately the result of luck, and only indirectly that of the skill, ability or effort of the player. For example, all three of Samuel Eto'o's goals scored against Manchester

United in the 2013–14 season were lucky. It was because of a massive deflection, being in the right place at the right time and the ball dropping at his feet directly in front of an undefended goal that explained most of how he scored his hat-trick. Without those slices of luck, that is, circumstances beyond his control that contributed to his scoring the goals, Chelsea might have drawn or lost the match, depending on how lucky Manchester United were. If you pay attention to the lead up to any goal in a football match, nearly all goals are due to luck to some extent, regardless of how strong or worthy the scoring team is.

The good things in life depend mostly on luck. Whether you have skill or not depends on luck. One person has a parent who takes them to football matches regularly, whereas another's family demands they work or study. One person has a wise, kind and encouraging coach, whereas another has an ignorant, cynical and belittling coach. Further, for a young player, the skill they develop and their level of motivation depend on many things outside themselves, for example, helpful parents, good coaches and conducive life circumstances. I could mention many other factors, which together make up the difference between a person becoming a Messi or a player on the worst team in the worst amateur competition.

This principle applies to all the external goods in life. For example, the beauty of a person, with which the person usually identifies, is not the result of hard work; it is a genetic gift of fortune. Thus, supermodels are among the luckiest people on the planet. In the sphere of education, employment and business, luck always has a crucial role to play. When there is more than one equally talented person applying for the same job, school, football club or whatever, how does the employer, selection panel or coach decide who to choose? The answer is personal preference, which is up to the judge, not the applicant.

The success of a person must involve luck, since a human being does not control all the causes that produced their success. Even the hard work that contributed to the success is due to luck, for we must be motivated to work. Motivation, or the desire to act or work, is not something entirely within our power. Our motivation is influenced by many things outside ourselves that we do not control. Not even the smartest psychologists can satisfactorily explain human motivation. And, if we are honest, most of us have no idea what really causes us to be motivated to do something.

We should acknowledge the role of luck in the achievement of success and the attainment of the goods of life. This can remove the unjustified additional source of pride that lies in the belief of a person that all their success was up to them. It is also a source of consolation for those of us who miss out on getting what they want in life or do not get to live their dreams exactly as they envision them. So, yes, successful people are extremely lucky.

On the other hand, without effort, hard work, commitment and the attempt to achieve your goals, no amount of luck will get you what you want. Paradoxically, to be motivated to work at all also requires luck. In any case, without luck your efforts will not get you what you want or lead you to your desired destination.

5

TRUTH AND REALITY EXIST

SOME PEOPLE SAY truth does not exist. Judgement, decision-making and our claims are merely matters of opinion. However, in football and life some opinions are closer to the truth than others. Obviously, this implies that truth exists. I will show that we have good reasons for believing that truth and reality exist.

Imagine an Arsenal player tackles a Chelsea player and does not touch the ball at all. It is likely that the Chelsea player, and all his teammates and fans, will interpret the challenge as a foul. The Arsenal player, his teammates and fans will probably say it was a fair challenge. Some Chelsea and Arsenal players and fans might take the opposite view to their own sides. But, in general, the players and fans will be blinded by their prejudice or desire to win. Their desire to win distorts their perception of what really happened.

To avoid bias, an impartial referee is authorised to control the game. A good referee is highly trained, has a perfect understanding of the rules and good judgement. The referee's objective judgement is closer to the truth than that of most of the players and fans because the referee wants to perform the role well. Fans are usually prejudiced and are not really interested in the objective application of the rules to an incident in a football match.

Many of our own judgements are poorly supported opinions. A good habit to form is to question your own opinions and judgements. Ask yourself what beliefs, desires or preferences you have that might colour your perception. By becoming aware of your biases and consciously removing them, you will make better judgements, that is, judgements closer to the truth. Likeminded people will recognise your attempt to be objective and uninfluenced by prejudice. These people will respect and trust you more and they will be more willing to rely on you, reward you with opportunity or take your views seriously.

Forming good judgements is difficult. Even though it can be hard to judge well, we should not conclude that there is no correct judgement or that one judgement cannot be closer to the truth or fairer than another. We know that the opinion of the facts of a judge is usually closer to the truth than the opinions of a plaintiff and a defendant. A judge's decision tends to be fairer than the judgements of adversaries in a court of law. The creation of computers, smart phones, aeroplanes and atomic weapons show that there is a real world that human beings understand and manipulate. Finally, Tilly Smith's 'opinion' or perception that a tsunami was coming was closer to the truth than her parents' opinions (discussed in chapter 18).

Most people who say all statements or judgements are nothing more than opinion tend to be insecure people riddled with doubt, which makes it difficult for them to form confident judgements. Consequently, they project their insecurity and doubt onto others. The rest of the sceptics think they are clever because they doubt everything, including themselves. They cannot commit to any claim because they fear what they say might smack of truth.

The ancient Greek philosopher Plato observed that it is easy to criticise the arguments of others and hard to provide a satisfactory account of things. The people we should admire are the ones who try to understand the world and share their understanding with us. In contrast with sceptics, those who are committed to living in reality are the strongest and most resilient because their actions and beliefs are guided by results and things that actually exist. It is only by living in accord with reality that we can form realistic plans and achieve real, positive outcomes in life. Have faith in your ability to reason well and try your best to form true or good judgements.

PART TWO

ETHICS

IN MODERN LIFE, the idea of ethics is understood to be about the moral rules that we should follow. On this understanding, ethics is just another name for morality. Certain ancient philosophers understood ethics to mean the theory of how to live a good life. Living a good life involved being morally good and living well. They believed that human wellbeing and moral goodness were inseparable. Plato, Aristotle, the Stoics and Spinoza conceived ethics in this way. This is what I mean by the word *ethics* in this book. Ethics is both about living the best kind of life you possibly can and complying with reasonable rules that are for the benefit of all. Playing football or life well or beautifully is to play it ethically.

PART TWO

ETHICS

6

WITH RULES, HARMONY; WITHOUT RULES, DISHARMONY

IMAGINE THERE WERE no rules in football, only players, a ball and goal posts. It would be chaos. A player could pick the ball up with their hands whenever they wanted, obstruct an opposing player without fear of giving away a free kick, always stand in the 6-yard box without fear of being called offside and perform a Maradona 'Hand of God' without fear of criticism or punishment. The absence of rules would also affect players' relationships with their teammates. The idea of a team involves the implicit rule that those who have been appointed to a team will work with the team to win the match. But, if there were no rules, a player could swap teams at any moment or pass the ball to an opponent and then change sides. Claims of loyalty would be questionable because people would do whatever they perceived to be advantageous to themselves.

This kind of game might be interesting for a little while, but eventually spectators and players would lose interest and become impatient. There needs to be order, otherwise we feel lost and out of control. We would ask: what is the point? If there were no order, scoring a goal would depend on the whims of each player. We couldn't hope for a ball to be passed or struck correctly because there would be no rule or principle that would guide the player with the ball. There could be dangerous challenges at any moment because there would be no rule against it and no referee to enforce the rule. Eventually, players would give up playing and spectators would give up spectating.

Rules give order to the game of football. They allow us to make plays and enable us to rationally anticipate what people on the pitch will do. For example, if you pass the ball to a teammate, they will strive to score a goal for your team, they may pass the ball back to you and together you would try to win the match. If a player scraped their studs down your shin while going for the ball at your feet, you would get a free kick and the other player would probably get a yellow or red card. Players wouldn't be able to always sit in the 6-yard box, which means their teammates wouldn't be able to hit a long ball every time to them to score a goal. There would have to be interplay in the middle of the pitch and players would have to watch the offside trap. So, not only do rules keep order, they protect you and others and promote positive aspects of the game.

Suppose there were no human made rules and no authority to enforce them. Life would be, as the English philosopher Thomas Hobbes described, 'solitary, poor, nasty, brutish, and short'. Human beings need rules and values to guide not only how football is played, but how the game of life is played. As I explained earlier, the idea of a team implies the principle of loyalty, which is also implied by the notions of citizenship, friendship and family. However, if there were no rules, then loyalty would be non-existent because everyone would focus only on trying to preserve themselves, at the expense of others if need be.

Without rules, your possessions could be forcibly taken from you and your rights would be unprotected. A stronger person or a group of people might take from you whatever you made or obtained through your own efforts or they could just kill you.

What if there were no rule that you must pay taxes? You might think that would be a good thing. But, the problem is your taxes help pay the police to protect you, your family and property. So, if there were no rules at all, you could not appeal to the police to protect you from attack or theft by others. If there were no rules at all, there would be anarchy.

In the same way that the rules make the game of football orderly and harmonious, the rules that govern human life ensure that it is orderly and harmonious. You might object that life is full of disorder and disharmony. It is hard to deny that. We should remember that there are degrees of order and that, insofar as there are rules and people follow them, there is order. Sometimes people ignore the rules or there is no 'referee' available to enforce them. And occasionally the referee (for example, the police or a judge) makes a bad call, in other words doesn't apply the rule correctly, and so people feel they have suffered injustice.

Nevertheless, if we want to produce order and harmony in social life, we need to have and obey good rules, and we need good judges to apply the rules. In football, people violate the rules usually because they are desperate, frustrated or because they want to exert their power. Likewise, people in society break the law because they are desperate, frustrated or feel the need to dominate and make people treat them like an important person. If we are to curtail these kinds of behaviours, we need rules and authorities to apply them.

This is an important principle because many of us just accept that there are rules and that we should obey them. Fewer people think about what the rules are for and what life would be like if there were no rules. Wise people, those who do think about and understand what rules are for, respect and follow the rules because they understand their purpose. This is why Aristotle said, 'I do without being commanded, what others do from fear of the laws.' Even though there are unjust rules and bad judges, we should accept that the rules are for our benefit. We should all follow the rules and help to make them more just. We can try to inspire people to be better judges and encourage others, mainly through our own example, to respect and follow the rules.

7

A RULE HAS FORCE ONLY IF ITS VIOLATION IS NOTICED

IN AN OFFICIAL football match, there is a referee to enforce the rules. We ordinarily think that we will be penalised if we break a rule. However, if the referee does not see a foul, it will not be punished. Perhaps the perpetrator will be punished by their conscience, if they have one. At any rate, the referee must witness the violation for the rule to operate.

The rules of football and the laws of a state are made and enforced by human beings. They are not imposed on us by supernatural judges who monitor our actions; nor are they invisible forces that snap into reality whenever a rule is violated, whereas natural laws, like the law of universal gravitation, always apply.

People generally act and feel as if human made rules are natural laws. A person who considers parking in a no-parking space, for example, often fears that the authorities are watching. We fear that as soon as we have violated the rule we will be punished. This is not how human made rules work. If the police or the authorities do not know of an offence, it will go unpunished.

It is important to realise this because, once you do, you will quickly see that rules come from you, me and other human beings. If we are the creators of the rules, then we can change them. There need not be a limit to the number of substitutions a team can make in a game. We need not have a law against smoking marijuana. These rules or laws come from us. We need to understand or remind ourselves that we have the power to determine the rules or laws that govern us.

The police and other authorities are not always watching over our shoulders. Once, when the local council was upgrading the road on my street, council workers helped me push my car onto the nature strip because it was in the way of their work. At the time, I did not know that my car could not be parked there. It remained parked there for over a month. Then, one day, I saw an expiation notice attached to the windscreen on my car. I wrote a letter explaining that council workers had helped me move the car there. The Council waived the fine.

The thing to notice, though, is that the rule against parking on the nature strip was ineffective until someone recognised its violation. Even the council workers who pushed my car did not know (or forgot) it was illicit to park my car on the nature strip. This shows that human rules are not things that exist independently of human beings. They are ideas in the human mind. Nevertheless, we cannot disobey rules and laws whenever we desire, for there is a complex system of authority and law-making that ensures the rules are applied when someone observes their violation.

It is worth contrasting the impartial approach of the law of a state with the approach of friends policing themselves. When you play a game of football with your friends, without a referee, you and your friends enforce the rules and you are likely to happily alert your friends to your own violations. You would do this because there is goodwill between you and your friends. This suggests that we do not need an authority to enforce all social rules.

THE BEAUTIFUL GAME

A hopeful thought is that, if we all played the game of life as we do when we play football with friends, there would be no need for the police, the courts or the army to enforce the rules. We would alert each other to our violations, we would not demand severe penalties, express animosity, and let anger and hatred infect our performance. We would recognise the violation, give the free kick and continue playing the game.

8

FOR THERE TO BE A WINNER, THERE MUST BE A LOSER

ONLY ONE TEAM can win the World Cup. There must be thirty-one losers. Even the runner-up is a loser. Not only will it hurt that they got so close to winning the competition only to fail, but that they made it to the final indicates their desire was very strong. Frustration of a strong desire causes profound sadness. For one team to experience elation, many must experience pain.

This is also true in the other parts of our lives. For every person who wins the lottery, gets the job, gains admission to a prestigious school or university or wins the heart of another person, someone else who also wanted it must miss out. In our society, in which we promote competition for these things, there must be many losers. That means for every person who gets the job, the girl or guy, or the reward, there is at least one and sometimes hundreds who must experience frustration and pain. The more intense their desire for the thing they wanted, the more intense their suffering.

The harm that fierce competition causes in contemporary societies is hidden, ignored or trivialised. But, the praise and celebration of the winners in life is normal and to be expected. The following principle explains this attitude. According to the English philosopher Jeremy

Bentham, 'Nature has placed mankind under the governance of two sovereign masters, *pain* and *pleasure*.' Failure makes us feel pain, whereas success makes us feel pleasure. We tend to avoid the former and gravitate to the latter. So, it is natural for human beings to focus on successful people in life and avoid discussing those who have failed.

It's like a family photo album. We display the photos in which we are smiling and look happy and leave out any in which we look miserable. Similarly, we glorify the winners, bestow upon them honours, attention and approval and quickly forget the contributions of the losers. At most, the losers get 'I'm sorry', 'good try' or 'bad luck', and are left to suffer their grief alone, with little or no sympathy.

What is lacking is compassion. Admittedly, the winners in a final of a tournament usually shake the hands of their opponents and sometimes even show empathy. However, that moment tends to be quickly forgotten and replaced by images of the celebration of the winners. Later, the winners are remembered and revered, whereas the losers are usually forgotten.

An alternative approach is to provide a more satisfying expression of commiseration, thoughtful feedback, reassurance and acknowledgement of the efforts and abilities of the players who fell short. We should not be afraid to acknowledge the role of luck too. This would make us feel more connected to each other. All of us have hopes and dreams and a need to be consoled and encouraged.

Competition cannot be eliminated from life. It's part of human nature and has been behind many of humanity's greatest achievements. The race to put humankind on the moon is a good example. Competition, if played in a respectful spirit, is fun. If you win, enjoy your victory and acknowledge those who helped you succeed. You can also offer friendship to your opponent, thank them for the competition, and acknowledge their courage, determination and ability. By doing so, you relieve, however little, some of their suffering and you elevate your own character.

9

THE JERSEY HAS THE POWER TO UNITE AND TO DIVIDE

FOOTBALL GENERATES STRONG emotions in fans of the game. Our emotions are connected to our thoughts about football. We see ourselves as supporters of a football club or our national team. The other teams in the competition are our opponents. We want the team we support to win and the opposing team to lose. As a player, we identify with the team or club we play for and see the other team's players as opponents. Some of us perceive them to be our enemies. Where there is a foul or a violation of a rule, most of us almost always take the side of the team we play for or support. This means that our loyalty is more important to us than our respect for the rules or for the *people* wearing the opposition uniforms.

Imagine a player wearing an opposition jersey swaps it for your team jersey, a common occurrence these days. And suppose that prior to the switch of jersey, the opponent unfairly tackled your teammate. Your opponent's foul would have angered you. After switching jersey, however, the feeling will probably go away. So, it's not really the person, but the jersey they are wearing, and our ideas associated with it, that most determine our emotional responses to unfair challenges and rule violations.

What this shows is that we treat the markings on a shirt as more real and important than the people wearing them. Doesn't that seem crazy to you? It's an accident that you were born in a particular area or country. The club or country you support or play for is not connected to you in an essential way. We often act as though we were born with our loyalty for club or country. The symbols and colours of the club or country we support are accidentally connected to our ideas about ourselves and what matters to us. Our loyalty is a matter of our emotions and how they have been conditioned.

Let's say you are a fan of Liverpool. Perhaps one of your parents is a Liverpool supporter and your love for them, which makes you love the things they love, caused you to love Liverpool and the things associated with it. If it wasn't your parent, it might have been a friend, or the television, because you had a strong positive feeling connected with witnessing Liverpool win the UEFA Champions League. This explains your future allegiance to Liverpool.

This is disconcerting because it shows that our loyalty to a club is due to chance. What if your parents had been Manchester United supporters? Perhaps the Liverpool fan will retort that they and their parents were born in Liverpool. Fair enough, and yet, such a response does not make as much sense as it used to.

Examination of the rise of Chelsea will reveal why the above response is deficient. When I started supporting Chelsea, it was not a serious contender for the English Premier League title. I did not know at the time that it had just won the FA Cup. I didn't even know what the FA Cup was. I chose Chelsea because a friend of mine who I looked up to was a Chelsea fan. About six years after I started following the club, the billionaire Roman Abramovich bought it.

This event catapulted Chelsea to success. The next season Chelsea finished second behind undefeated Arsenal, its highest position since it was champion of the First Division in 1954–55. Chelsea won the next two Premier League titles in a row and from then on was constantly challenging for the title. Naturally, given its success, there have been a lot of bandwagon jumpers. Now we can ask: who are the real Chelsea fans?

The obvious answer is the people who were born in or grew up in Chelsea. Because they grew up here and followed Chelsea all their lives, they are supposedly the real Chelsea fans and the rest are fake fans. We can now ask: what is it about the club that is local to Chelsea other than its geographical location?

The club is owned by a billionaire foreigner. Nearly all the players are from places outside England, let alone Chelsea. It is a business, not primarily a group of individuals representing a community. Its representatives openly talk about gaining a bigger share of the football fan market, which shows that it is about making money more than being a local identity. That the club is based in Chelsea is now incidental to the corporate nature and activity of the club. This applies to virtually all professional football clubs that import foreign players and promote their team brand to people outside the geographical location of the club.

The money invested in Chelsea has given rise to its success. The so-called true fans are really supporting a business run by a foreigner, its players are mostly foreigners, and it is predominantly for the sake of foreigners. Most people outside Chelsea support the club because of its success and marketing. This applies to all the big clubs. That is why the famous clubs are advertised and go on tours around the world.

Yet, underneath the club badge and colours are human beings who could be wearing another badge or colours tomorrow. There was a time when most players played for one club for their entire professional careers. Now, the fans and even the players are confused. Consider Frank Lampard who played for West Ham United, Chelsea and then

Manchester City, two big rivals of Chelsea. Cesc Fàbregas signed for Chelsea from Barcelona, having made his name at Arsenal, one of Chelsea's biggest rivals in the Premier League.

The ease with which players can be transferred often results in confusion and interesting consequences. Lampard's performance for Manchester City against Chelsea in the 2014–15 Premier League season is a good representative case. Both the City and Chelsea fans applauded Lampard when he was substituted into the game in the seventy-eighth minute. He was on the pitch for only seven minutes when he scored his first goal for the club and rescued a point for City. Having played for the Blues for most of his career and being one of its best players, the fans couldn't hate Lampard, especially since Chelsea had decided not to renew his contract and had let him leave as a free agent. Lampard's feat is unusual because he had helped City at the expense of Chelsea, but he had been a Chelsea player for thirteen years and he is the club's record leading goal-scorer. Understandably, at the end of the match Lampard was applauded by both sets of fans.

This kind of confusion is prevalent at the national level too. There are many examples of players switching sides and playing for a country other than the one they were born in. It's understandable that many countries are happy to naturalise Brazilian footballers. Even Spain adopted the Brazilians Marcos Senna (who helped them win the 2008 UEFA European Football Championship) and Diego Costa. Perhaps one day Brazil will, in reality, win every World Cup because every national team will be filled with naturalised Brazilians.

More confusing is the situation involving the Boateng brothers, Jérôme and Kevin-Prince. The former plays for Germany and the latter played for Ghana before his international career stalled. They played on opposite teams at the 2010 World Cup. This kind of example challenges what it means to identify yourself as a citizen of a country, and even what it means to be a member of a family. This should make us wary of caring too much about the colours of the shirt or symbol attached to the clothing of a person.

It's unwise to take too seriously football clubs and countries and the symbols and colours associated with them. We need to be aware of the power symbols have over us, which can blind us to the reality of a situation, for example, that two players on opposing teams are brothers. Let's become aware of the way in which these symbols are affecting us, for then we can get rid of their power over us. This will enable us to see things on the park as they are, which is human beings trying to get a ball into the back of a net.

There is nothing wrong with having teams and distinguishing them by different colours and symbols. It's fun to play team football. I play with a group of guys and we change teams regularly. We all know each other, and we don't really care who is on whose team if it's fair and competitive.

Some people don't perceive football in this open-minded way. There are people who have a gang mentality about club colours and symbols. They identify supporters of other clubs as the enemy. This attitude has given rise to violence, racism and hatred. People with this kind of mindset are oblivious to the power these symbols have over them. They are unaware that symbols don't represent any substantial similarities or differences between the people wearing them. Blindness to the power of symbols over us is a dangerous thing. Yet, once we are aware of it, they will have little power over us and we can still enjoy team sports.

Symbols and badges are common in most areas of human life. They influence religion (the Cross of Christ), business (Nike logo), politics (the swastika) and culture (Google). Symbols pervade society and influence us subconsciously. Of course, a symbol can mean different things to different people. The Christian Cross enrages some people because they associate it with thoughts about the Crusades, the Inquisition or child abuse, while others associate it with love, the one true God and the saviour of humankind.

Brand names are another kind of symbol that can affect us. A good example is the name 'Michael Jordan'. The name 'Jordan' represents a business that is worth billions of dollars. Even now the name 'Jordan', associated with arguably the greatest basketballer of all time, is enough to get people to pay a lot of money for items associated with this name. When I was younger, I got a nod of respect just because I was wearing Jordan clothing. At the height of his fame, some kids were violently robbed or even killed for their Jordan shoes. This kind of tragedy still occurs today. In 2017, a teenager was apparently killed for his pair of Air Jordan sneakers. This shows that a symbol has the power to make some people want to kill.

A national flag is a different kind of powerful symbol. Seeing the Australian national flag inspires many Australians to be patriotic and can make them cry, and damaging or burning the flag is likely to anger them and make them want to punish the perpetrators. On the other hand, some people see the flag as representing oppression and the blind following of authority, so it evokes the feeling of disgust. I am not interested in commenting on which interpretation of these symbols is correct or valid. My aim is to highlight the enormous power of symbols to influence us. Many of us let these symbols influence us without realising it. It is better to see symbols for what they are, so that we can take back the power they have over us.

10

THE GOOD OF THE INDIVIDUAL DEPENDS ON THE GOOD OF THE TEAM

A GOOD FOOTBALLER can flourish only on a good team. A team of incompetent or selfish players makes it difficult for an individual to shine. Strong opposition will overwhelm the individual's attempts to make a difference in the game. If your opponent knows that you won't pass the ball—for example, because you try to beat their team all by yourself whenever you have it at your feet—you become predictable and easier to dispossess.

On a team of competent and cooperative players, an individual has more opportunities to affect the outcome of the match. If you mix your one-on-one ability with engaging your teammates, then you become less predictable and you are more likely to get the ball into your attacking area of the pitch. A good team makes you better because your teammates will make intelligent runs, pass the ball when they should and can get the ball to you.

The better each player fulfils their role, the stronger the team and the more likely its success. A Socceroos player said Australia was impressive in the 2006 World Cup because Guus Hiddink, the manager, ensured that every player knew their role and performed the duties connected to it as well as they could. Australia was highly competitive at the 2006

World Cup and were unfortunate not to progress further than the round of 16.

One might object that emphasis on the excellence of the team might overshadow a player's abilities and individuality. But, is that so bad? What is more important: taking a risk by showing off and possibly hurting your team, or fulfilling your role as well as you can for the sake of your team? Players who always want to be the star on the team often lose possession, which causes additional pressure for teammates or results in the concession of a goal. Selfish actions hurt the team and disappoint the fans.

You can be a team player and try to exercise your creativity wisely, but service to the team should be your main priority. Even when you decide to be creative, your act of creativity should be aimed at helping the team, for by doing so, your desire to win the match is more likely to be satisfied.

One of the characteristics that has enabled human beings to dominate the Earth and all the other animals is intelligent cooperation. Human cooperation makes amazing feats possible. I have seen documentary footage of three Maasai men, armed only with bows and arrows and knives, walk up to a group of fifteen feasting lions. They scared the lions away and took their food. Teamwork and intelligence enabled them to do this. The unity of the Maasai men was crucial. Each one had to believe the other was totally committed to, and focused on, the goal. Imagine if one of them tried to impress the others by attempting to take the food from the lions alone? The lions probably would have killed and eaten him.

Human cooperation allows most us to live free from fear of attack by natural predators, and have readily accessible food, shelter and other conveniences of life. The problem is that this kind of cooperation is disinterested. That is, people cooperate without realising and caring that they are doing so. The shopkeeper cooperates with us when selling us food and we cooperate when we pay for it. Without cooperation we could not enjoy the convenience of getting food without having to grow or produce it ourselves. Most of the time we take this kind of cooperation for granted.

Disinterested cooperation results from a lack of empathy and sense of connectedness to other people. It is like being on a football team where players do not really care about what happens after they pass the ball and are uninterested in the outcome of the match. Footballers like this are self-absorbed.

Self-absorption is common in modern societies. Social media, YouTube and smart phones breed self-absorption. What is lacking is real communities in which people interact face-to-face, feel related to each other and are unafraid to be themselves. We need to understand or remind ourselves that we depend on each other for our survival and wellbeing.

In football, the goal is victory. Cooperation with our teammates is the best way to further that goal. Similarly, if we want to win the greatest prize of human life, which is to live joyfully, then we must do it together. Sure, individuals have the right to pursue their own goals and try to realise their dreams, but an individual can also make an empathetic and meaningful contribution to the team of humanity.

11

THE 'UNSUNG HEROES' ARE JUST AS VALUABLE AS THE SUPERSTARS

IN FOOTBALL, IT is usually the attacking players who get the accolades and most of the attention. They usually score the goals that win the games that cause people to be deliriously happy or sad. Also, the flicks, tricks and spectacular goals excite the imagination and thrill the fans, which is what most people want. Defensive players and goalkeepers tend to take a backseat to the hype that surrounds the attacking players. The player of the season or the World Player of the Year is nearly always an attacking player.

In victorious teams, defensive players and goalkeepers tend to not get the glory and honour they deserve in comparison to the attacking players. This is because our imaginations are stronger than our desire to understand and appreciate the game. James Rodríguez's goal against Uruguay in the round of 16 of the 2014 World Cup enraptured football fans around the world. By contrast, the defence of Costa Rica, which was so good that it enabled them to escape the 'group of death' (England, Italy and Uruguay) and reach the quarter finals with one of the worst attacks in the competition, appeared to impress only football analysts. For most fans, the achievement of Costa Rica was overshadowed by the exploits of players like James, Neymar and Messi.

I'm not suggesting we should ignore the brilliant skills of attacking players, but we should become more discerning and appreciative of the skills and efforts of goalkeepers and defensive players. If you are a defensive player or goalkeeper, you need to be aware of this and remind yourself that your role is crucial to the success of your team.

There are numerous stars and brilliant individuals in life. We admire and respect musicians, actors, authors, public personalities, sports stars, multi-millionaires and billionaires, entrepreneurs and businesspeople. We aspire to be like them and they are often the topic of our conversations.

The opposite is true when we discuss people in less eye-catching professions and roles in society. The people who really are the most important are doctors, nurses, teachers and farmers. Farmers, doctors and nurses are essential for the preservation of the body and educators are necessary for the liberation and empowerment of the human mind.

Teachers have a high status in countries like China. The Chinese people understand that teachers are essential for educating their students about the world, be it in the area of medicine, technology or science. This might be why the Chinese tend to score highly in academic tests but tend to do poorly in football on the international stage!

Later in the book I will discuss the principle that knowledge is power. The value of teachers is related to this principle. Teachers are a source of knowledge. Therefore, teachers are a source of human power. Since human beings want power, it makes sense to seek out the best teachers and celebrate their contributions to humanity. Sometimes the service of teachers is recognised and publicly honoured. But, even when we do acknowledge the efforts of teachers, we give them minimal attention compared with what the dazzling people have lavished upon them. So, why is it that we praise the dazzling people more than the essential ones?

Dazzling people more easily evoke strong emotions in us. In football, dispossessing a player can evoke a feeling of joy, but unless it's a game-saving tackle, the feeling is likely to be weak and fleeting. By contrast, a 30-yard strike that bends around a wall and flies into the top corner excites the imagination and produces in us feelings of awe and intense joy. The intensity can be so great that often the image of the goal being scored will not leave us for quite a while.

Likewise, the seemingly universal high that arose from Barack Obama becoming President of the United States and the apparently universal depression surrounding Donald Trump winning the presidency dominated the minds of people around the world. Movie stars like Bruce Lee stoked frenzied admiration from fans, especially in China, and pop music stars like Justin Bieber inspire the imaginations of many admirers. The media likes to focus on billionaires and their lifestyles, like Richard Branson and Bill Gates. It is not hard to understand why, since most of us want what the rich and the famous have, but it is also because of the way they make us feel, such as the charisma of Bruce Lee or Obama, which inspire us with hope and wonder.

What we talk about most often or enthusiastically indicates what we ordinarily value, care about or desire most. Our inordinate focus on the rich and famous indicates that most of us value wealth, fame and glory above everything else. This is inconsistent with what we really care about most, namely, our wellbeing, which includes the health of our bodies and the development of our minds.

Emerson wrote that the first principle of true wealth and power is health, and Aristotle observed that all people desire to understand. Understanding ourselves, the world and the games we play is one of the highest goods for a human being. If we want to maximise these values in our own and each other's lives, we should give more attention to, and care more about, the role and value of healthcare professionals, educators and generally people in professions that daily contribute to the promotion of health, understanding and, ultimately, human wellbeing.

12

ABILITY COMPELS RESPECT

RESPECT IS IMPORTANT for a footballer. This statement is multifaceted, since there are at least three kinds of respect. There is the respect you give a player simply because they are a fellow human being. This means that you don't insult, degrade, humiliate or do anything that makes the player feel inferior as a human being. There is the respect that involves understanding the abilities of your opponents and teammates and performing your skills in accord with that understanding. That is, you don't underestimate your opponents' or teammates' abilities. Underestimation is usually caused by overestimating your own ability. Then there is the respect you receive because you have ability. I will discuss the last kind of respect here, but a point about the second kind is worth mentioning. The first goes without saying.

As a competent player, you might believe another player is less skilled than you. You might let your guard down, but even with your opponent's modest ability, they might go past you and score a goal that defeats your team. The same goes for life. It's unwise to underestimate other people. Everyone will know something you don't. If you spend eight hours a day developing your football skills, and another spends that time learning the law, medicine or art, they will know, or be able to do, something that you don't or can't, and vice versa. The problem with some people is that they become good at something and mistakenly think they are good at everything. They then look down on others, but only a fool fails to respect the abilities of other people.

The respect you receive because of the ability you have is crucial to success in football and life. In football, if you have ability, your teammates are much more likely to give you the ball when you call for it. Your opponents are likely to be tentative, if they know you have ability. Skilful footballers make their opponents stand off from them. The opposition is extremely cautious when Messi, Cristiano Ronaldo, Neymar or Hazard is attacking them with the ball at their feet. They are hesitant and usually foul them or make an error that allows the attacking player to hurt their team.

Respect for your ability may transfer to you as a person. Superstar footballers are often asked for their opinion on how to live, eat, dress, on politics and so on, even though they might know little or nothing about these matters. Nevertheless, in the sphere of football the respect and interest in who you are and what you say begins with demonstrated footballing ability.

We should not blame others for their lack of respect for our abilities as footballers, for the principle that *ability compels respect* is an inviolable natural law and a principle of causality. Respect is the effect of a cause, namely, ability. If the cause is not given, the effect cannot follow.

Conversely, if you have ability, respect must follow. A kitten does not cause us to tremble because we perceive that it has little power to destroy us. But, an adult lion easily intimidates us because we know that its natural power dwarfs our own. Real ability or power is undeniable and earns respect. So, a footballer who is not respected must have limited ability. A player who lacks ability and respect should think of himself or herself as a lion cub that has the potential to one day be king of the game of football or life.

In life, the ability to communicate well determines whether you, your views and your values will be respected by other people. The ability to relate to other people and the ability to empathise are also crucial. Good friendships, romantic and other kinds of relationships are possible only if you have strong communication and social skills. Individuals with these skills are respected by other people.

Respect is essential in the workplace too. Without ability, there will be little or no respect. Where there is no respect, work can be depressing. However, having ability in your workplace will attract respect from your colleagues, even if they are ambitious and envious of you. Your superiors will likely recognise your ability and respect you because of it. Advancement in your workplace is likely to result.

A person who wants to do well in football or life must develop their abilities. Only then will a person be respected. By striving to increase our ability and thereby gaining respect from others, we will find it easier to persuade others to cooperate with us and assist us to achieve our goals.

PART THREE
DESIRE, LOVE AND PASSION

EMOTIONS ARE ESSENTIAL to human life. Desire, love and passion are known to everyone, even though they differ in terms of what they are associated with, as are their strength and prevalence in each of our lives. What motivates us is connected to our desires, our loves, passions and dreams. By understanding our emotions, we can better understand motivation and how to accomplish our goals.

13

WHOEVER WANTS THE BALL MOST IS MOST LIKELY TO GET IT

WHAT IS THE difference between a great footballer like Messi and a player who hasn't had as much success? *Desire*, is the answer, *strength* of desire, to be more precise. There are many other factors that contribute to a footballer's success, but strength of desire is the most important one. You might object that you desire to play football as much as anyone else, but you don't play for your national team or Barcelona.

Let us examine your objection. How can we measure the strength of a desire? The strength of your desire is evident in your actions. Messi and other famous footballers have usually played football from an early age. They have played football for many hours, every day, for many years. In that time, their skills have continually improved, their understanding and ability to play the game have increased, and their confidence has risen steeply. All these qualities arose from their powerful desire to play football.

Messi has spent considerably more time than most developing his skills and playing football. Another individual may play football once or twice a week and love every second of it. In addition to playing football, this person may study or read a lot of books, play another sport and learn a martial art. Messi focused most of his attention on playing football. So, Messi's ability is much greater than the ability of most other footballers. Perhaps that is why Messi plays for Barcelona and another person plays for their local club.

The above comparison highlights the consequences of strong desire. Desire has cumulative effects. All the hours of playing prior to a game, time spent doing what someone like Messi wanted to do, are translated into better touch, fewer mistakes and improved ability to read the game. This footballing experience, together with the strong desire in a game, combine to make Messi a formidable footballer. The strength of your desire to play largely determines the level of success you can attain in the beautiful game.

In life, as in football, there are many factors that determine how successful you will be and what you get in life. Some people are born with advantages. They are born into wealth, born beautiful, or born to parents who lovingly provide support, resources, a good example and education. These qualities by themselves won't lead a person to success. Without a strong and persistent desire, you will not have a good relationship. Without a strong and persistent desire, you will not achieve and maintain professional success. Without a strong and persistent desire, you are not likely to get much or achieve much in life.

People do not magically achieve things in this world. A famous movie star, supermodel, a president or prime minister, a doctor or lawyer might seem special in some way. You see them as they are today. However, you haven't *witnessed* their personal history or their life experiences. Like Messi and other footballing greats, successful people in life intensely desired to be where they are today.

The time and effort they put into getting what they wanted was fuelled by a strong desire. Their desire led them to learn their trade, attend school or college, and to seek and take opportunities, not occasionally, but every day, again and again. Stephen King, the famous writer, read numerous books and wrote continually during his childhood and adolescence. He really wanted to read and become a writer. Writing 500 words once a month reflects weak desire (you are probably doing many other things you want to do), whereas King writes about 2,000 words a day, every day.

Consider a concert. Most people probably want to get as close to the stage as possible, so they can be near their favourite musician or performer. What separates those who get nearer to the stage from those who are stuck at the back? It is what people do. The people at the front usually arrive many hours before the concert starts because they really want to get a good position, as close to the stage as possible.

Another factor is that when you are close to the stage, people surround, shove, sweat on and push you. Some people feel uncomfortable in this kind of situation and *want* space and that is what they get when they move to a less populated area. They may say they want to be closer to the stage, but what they *really* want is to feel comfortable. The people who are close to the stage want to be nearer to their idol more than they want to feel comfortable.

This kind of behaviour occurs in football too. Footballers might say they want the ball but don't chase it because they don't want to feel the stress on the body that results from chasing the ball. A player who gets the ball thought less or not at all about the discomfort of running and competing and more about winning the ball and scoring a goal.

The people who most want the goods of life usually get them. They do so because they act despite the uncomfortable feelings they experience in the pursuit of whatever they want and their actions attract the object of their desire to them. You may want something, but do you really want it? Do you want it more than the next person? Do you want it more than the other things you want?

14

PASSION GIVES PURPOSE AND PURPOSE GIVES LIFE MEANING

A PASSION FOR football is common to fans of the game. It gives a player purpose, a reason to get up in the morning and something to look forward to in life. Your level of passion for football determines your level of interest in the game. Your passion determines what you do with your time, for example, training, practicing or playing football versus, say, watching another sport, a movie, going shopping or playing video games.

Your passion also determines how you identify yourself, for example, as a footballer, a striker, or a fan of a club or national team. Your passion for your club or country determines how you see the world. If you are an Australian, your passion for the Socceroos entails seeing other national teams and their fans as opponents. It follows that you must wish that they fail in order that the team you have a passion for will prevail. We can see, then, that passion is the source of meaning and purpose associated with the game of football.

There is a noticeable difference between passion in football and passion in life. Virtually everyone who is a fan of football passionately loves the game (to varying degrees), but the same cannot be truly said of all participants in the game of life. The opposite seems to be true. More people in life tend to lack passion for something than those who are blessed with a passion. A high school student said to me at the end of a philosophy class I gave: 'I wish *I* had a passion for something'. She was with about five other students who had come up to me after a speech I gave on the value of philosophy. Clearly, I had communicated my passion for philosophy to the students in the class. It's also clear that not everyone has a passion for something.

True, we all have our loves, likes and sources of joy. Few have a passion for life that is as strong and fulfilling as the passion of a football fan. In my experience, and from what numerous psychological and sociological studies suggest, many people are deprived not only of a passion, but also happiness or wellbeing. A lot of people suffer from mental disorders such as depression and anxiety. The World Health Organization predicts that by 2030 the most widespread health complaints will be depression and related mental illnesses. No wonder there are few people in the world who look forward to every new day as a footballer or fan does to match day.

How do we become passionate about life or anything for that matter? Here is a simplified theory of passion, derived from the philosophy of Spinoza, in my view the wisest and most admirable philosopher and human being to have ever lived—and I'm not alone. Einstein wrote a poem in which he expressed his esteem for Spinoza's wisdom and exemplary character. According to Bertrand Russell, a prominent philosopher of the 20th century, 'Spinoza is the noblest and most lovable of the great philosophers'.

According to Spinoza, you intensely love, or are passionate about, something when you experience joy and that feeling is brought about by, and associated with, an external cause or thing. For example, I play or watch football. I experience joy and my mind associates this with the idea of football. That is, playing or watching football (which involve external causes such as other players and the movement of the ball affecting my body) causes joy in me. Therefore, I love the game of football.

The stronger the experience of joy when I play or watch football, the more I love and want to watch or play football. So, it is our emotions, conditioned by things outside us, that determines both what we are passionate about and the degree of our passion.

Notice that this is a passive process. You can't force yourself to experience joy; it is something that happens to you. That is why it seems impossible to force yourself to be passionate about something or life. Since we have many times experienced sadness, accompanied by the *idea* of life itself as the cause of our sadness, it is easy to see why many of us would laugh at the idea of having a passion for life.

The solution to lacking a passion for something is to try new activities and develop new skills and knowledge. Football fans enjoy the game because they understand it and appreciate the skills of footballers. Footballers enjoy playing football, particularly when they perform a skill excellently. When a fan's team plays well, or a footballer performs well, they experience joy accompanied by the idea of watching or playing football.

We can become more passionate about our lives by engaging with the world and letting it and the people in it affect us emotionally. By doing so, we may discover a new source of joy that can make our lives more interesting and meaningful. If you are not yet passionate about something in life, it may be that you have restricted yourself to the familiar and comfortable. To live a more meaningful life we need to try new activities and be open to new experiences.

You might try a new activity for only a little while and then move on. Treat this not as failure to find something to be passionate about, but as a necessary step on the path to finding something that truly fills you with passion. Even if you don't find a passion, at least you will be more active and continually have new experiences that will make your life more interesting. New experiences can also present opportunities to make new friends or to find someone to share your life with.

15

MOTIVATION IS INITIATED AND SUSTAINED BY EXTERNAL THINGS

HAVE YOU EVER wondered what got you interested in football? If you support Barcelona, perhaps a family member was a Barcelona fan and watched or took you to Barcelona games. However, you might have a brother or sister who the family member did the same things with, but they either hate or are indifferent to football. What explains this difference between you and your sibling? In your case, the initial and subsequent football experiences evoked a strong feeling of joy in you, whereas in your sibling the joyful feeling was lukewarm, non-existent or they experienced a kind of pain (perhaps the ball hit them in the face or it was a boring game).

This shows us that our experiences, and not genetics or some inherent mental power, are what cause us to become football fans. Experience implies passivity, that is, we have been affected by things or events outside us. It is what happens to you or what you did in response to things or events that impacted you. Our experiences condition our emotions and our emotions determine what we do. So, our desires and loves are to a large extent determined by things external to us. In other words, our life experiences give rise to our motivations.

We do not motivate ourselves to play or watch football. The world, in the form of footballers and their actions, motivates us to play and love football. In my own case, I did not turn to myself and say, 'Now I will love football'. My love for the game arose from playing indoor football at school lunch breaks when I was about seventeen years old. The people I hung out with, most of them football fans, would go to the gymnasium to play. Naturally, I followed them.

The joy I *experienced* when I scored goals made me look forward to lunch break every school day. Some older students, who were passionate Premier League fans, fanned the flame of my love for football. They would discuss football and the Premier League, which, because I loved playing and they spoke about it with enthusiasm, made me want to watch the Premier League, too.

There were two dominant characters in our group, a Manchester United fan and a Liverpool fan. Both picked on supporters of rival clubs, especially the United fan. Because United were dominating and winning everything, my school mate's arrogance generated a very strong desire in me to see United lose. When they did lose, the feeling of joy accompanied with my making fun of my school mate gave rise to a strong desire to watch all United games in the hope of seeing an upset. Unfortunately, at the time United didn't lose many because they had an amazing team.

The experience of seeing on television the likes of Ronaldo (the Brazilian), Zinedine Zidane and Gianfranco Zola exhibit fantastic skills made me feel excited, and that excitement gave rise to my desire to emulate them. I sought information on how to develop football skills, listened to football commentators like Johnny Warren and Les Murray and read football skills magazines. I would watch very closely how Ronaldo and Zidane performed a crossover or pirouette and practice doing them. In relation to my love of football, whether it was watching or playing, what got me interested, kept me interested and moved me to watch, play and grow as a footballer was the intense joy I would feel when watching, playing or debating the game.

Why is one person more motivated than another to play or train, go to a game, watch or talk about football? The answer is simple. They have a strong desire to do so and they have this desire because they have experienced joy when watching or playing football. A problem for many people is that the initial experience might be boring or frustrating because there have been no goals, they have not been involved successfully in the game or they have desires connected to other things they enjoy. In addition, the psychological make-up of some people (for example, they love Australian Rules Football, or they love reading more than sports), shaped by different experiences, will make them resistant to being affected with joy by football. Thus, it won't always be possible to get people interested to play or watch football.

Nevertheless, the only way to motivate people to play or watch football is to make it as enjoyable as possible. There needs to be exciting action, involvement and a sense of connectedness, for example, to a club or country. This applies to training as well. Yes, hard work is important, and we can come to enjoy hard work, but training must be enjoyable. Ball work and practice matches are the most enjoyable parts of a training session and are most likely to keep people interested and motivate them to train.

This principle can be applied to any area of your life in which motivation is important. If you want to motivate yourself or other people to work harder, be more productive, take education seriously, improve fitness and health or take care of relationships, then you must evoke the *desire* in yourself or others to do so. This can be achieved by doing something relevant to your aim that will cause joy. Once you do this, you or the other people you are working with will associate the activity with joy. By establishing this association, you will be able to motivate yourself or someone else to do the activity by presenting to the mind (your own or another person's) something related to it. Things that trigger the association can be in the form of a person's own thoughts (perhaps imagining what they will look like when they have lost weight) or something external to them, for example, images on television, a book or seeing someone engaged in the activity (playing football, exercising or eating healthy food).

Many years ago, I read a full-page advertisement for the Spartan Health Regime (now Regimen) by Anthony Bova. This advertisement inspired me. It described what Bova calls the modern Spartan path, which he claims can produce perfect health, extraordinary strength and mental toughness. The image of myself becoming a modern Spartan warrior induced a strong feeling of joy in me. That joy gave rise to my desire to purchase the manual, which was about $150, a lot of money for me at the time, and something I had never done before.

I did not properly read the Spartan Health Regime until about two years after I purchased it. At the time I bought it, my life was a nightmare in many ways, which explains why I was attracted to the image of physical strength and power. It also explains why I did not actually follow the Spartan principles. However, when I finally escaped the hell I was living in, I followed the program.

It began with a friend's suggestion that we go for a run. His suggestion reminded me of the Spartan manual and made me return to it. This time I read it closely and applied the principles. I would exercise and go for a run nearly every day. I completely stopped drinking alcohol and almost always ate only healthy food. I achieved excellent results. I was lean, full of energy, proud and had high self-esteem. My training and healthy living naturally made me more attractive. A girl told me to put my shirt back on because she could not take her eyes off my body. It annoyed her because when I was younger she used to hate me. The important point, though, is that the excellent results were a source of joy, which is why I continued with the program.

Motivation is the desire to do something beneficial for *yourself*. Only when your desire is strong will your motivation be strong. Your desire will be strong if it arises from a high level of joy caused by an external thing. The key is to have external things in your environment that are a means of producing the joy that sustains or increases the strength of your desire. If you want to be motivated to live healthily, then imagery, presence of the right kind of foods, supportive friends and anything that is conducive to the fulfilment of your desire can contribute to maintaining motivation.

Alternatively, if you want to know what motivates you, take note of what causes joy in you. Pay attention to the things in your environment that make you feel good. That way, you can to some extent take control of what motivates you (for example, ensure the things that produce joy in you are continually present or remove things that are obstacles to producing joy in you). The greater control you have over the external things in your personal space, the more power you will have to produce and sustain 'self-motivation'.

16

THE HUMAN EGO IS A CHARMING SERPENT

THE FOOTBALL GODS inspire us to watch and play football. We hope to witness them create magic on the football pitch and we try to replicate their genius in our own game. Pele, Cruyff, Maradona, Cristiano Ronaldo, Messi and Zidane are footballing gods. We try to do the Cruyff Turn, the flick, the stepover, the backheel, the outside of the foot shot on goal, and the pirouette. Maradona's single-handed destruction of England in the 1986 World Cup and Zidane's stunning goal in the 2002 Champions League final have inspired millions of people to love football and to try to emulate their amazing skills.

The ego is responsible for us wanting to be the star. Everyone has an ego, whether they want to admit it or not. The ego is a person's self-concept, which is united to the desire to feel superior to other people. The desire to feel superior is necessary to our survival because it motivates us to do the things that will prolong our lives and preserve or increase our power. If we feel superior, we will compete for resources or advantage, but if we feel inferior, we usually avoid competition. This desire inheres in human nature, since, as Spinoza explains, every human being strives to preserve themselves and to maximise their natural power. As I explain in Chapter 20, the power by which human beings strive to preserve themselves can be understood as the instinct to self-preservation.

From this principle Spinoza concludes that humility and self-humiliation are very rare. The reason for this is that 'human nature, considered in itself, strives against them as much as it can; hence those, who are believed to be most self-abased and humble, are generally in reality the most ambitious and envious.'

This explains why footballers are inclined to be the star of the game, as opposed to a nobody. Most footballers learn to suppress their self-interested tendencies, but in some they remain dominant. We should not be too hard on these footballers, for Spinoza teaches us that egotism exists within every human being. The ego is central to a person's identity because it springs from their individual human nature, namely, the power by which they strive to preserve themselves and increase their power.

A star in football or life feels special. This is a highly effective way to satisfy a person's desire to feel and believe they are superior to others. The influence of the ego is evident when a player tries to take on the entire opposing team, takes a shot from 30-yards out or from an impossibly tight angle in the hope of scoring a wonder goal. From time to time it works, and people are awestruck. However, even the best players only occasionally score amazing goals or perform incredible passes, flicks or tricks. That is why they are called 'highlights'.

Players who want to be heroes and try something extraordinary sometimes pull it off and win the game. When they succeed, their moment of genius, even though it was motivated by the ego, makes the difference and inspires all those who witness it. The ego has a kind of charm that mesmerises us.

On the flipside, ego-motivated football can cause us to groan and cause a great deal of frustration. I've lost count how many times I've witnessed amateurs and professionals ignore an open player who had an easy tap-in. Instead, they try to beat another player after having beaten one or two, or they try to score a difficult goal, rather than pass the ball to an open player. It's obvious why they do it. They want to be the hero and have everything that goes along with it: the thrill of scoring a goal or beating their opponent, and the admiration, adulation and feeling that they are the star of the game.

There are consequences for allowing the ego too much control. If you keep hogging the ball and making mistakes, sooner or later your teammates will be reluctant to pass the ball to you and your coach will think seriously about relegating you to the bench. Ironically, most of the time the best footballers play the simple ball, albeit with great intensity and precision. When the great players do something amazing it is only one moment out of the numerous moments that make up the game.

The problem is that the moments of magic are put into highlights packages, and so they stick in the imagination. Consequently, we try to reproduce their brilliance in our own games. A focus on highlights alone can, and often does, distorts one's view of footballing ability. If you go to play the game with the expectation of doing something dazzling with the ball whenever it comes to you, you are likely to look foolish and make your teammates and fans angry with you.

Ultimately, if you are always focused on doing something wonderful, then you are driven by your ego more than your motivation to contribute to the team, which should be your principal focus if you want to win the match. Wonder goals are possible because of your teammates. A good pass from a teammate or dragging a defender away from you helps you to score a goal. So, neglect of your teammates is ignorant and selfish.

In any case, the glorification of individual players misrepresents the nature of football. There is nothing wrong with glorifying, admiring, and loving certain players and enjoying their brilliance. That is only one part of the game, though. If we want to see the beautiful game at its most beautiful, then we need to remind ourselves that it is a team game. The best teams usually win by playing as a team, and without a good team even the most talented footballer will have trouble shining, for they need to get the ball from someone. As the saying goes, *a great team will beat a team of great players*.

If you want to witness and enjoy the beautiful game of life, your ego should be put in the back seat and your desire to work with your fellow human beings should be your foremost motive. Where there are two or more people engaged in some activity, be it a meeting, working on a project, or planning some event, there is often someone who feels they have better skill, better understanding, or are simply better than the others. It might be true, but a good outcome is more likely to occur when everyone works together as a team. In the context of a team activity, if you try to do something on your own and mess up, you will look stupid, your colleagues will be furious with you and those who are invested in the outcome and employed you will demand responsibility and recompense.

Human nature is such that many of us want to be the centre of attention or outshine their friends, family or colleagues. This is calamitous in conversation. Intelligent people can charm us with their interesting and insightful conversation, but sometimes they try to appear smarter than everyone else, which is repulsive, and it can be a barrier to forming real and lasting friendships. Some people must finish every sentence, have the last say or be the one who argues best. This kind of vice is common in romantic relationships. Many people complain their date talked only about themselves and barely stopped for a few seconds to listen to the other person, only to impatiently return to sharing their own wonderful story.

This egotism comes at the expense of the value of other people. Another person might have something valuable or interesting to say, but because the ego wants to have the spotlight, it impels a person to impose its opinion on the other people present, even though they may not be in a good position to do so. In other words, rather than letting another who knows what they are talking about share their view, they say something tedious, which makes them look bad and annoys the participants in the conversation.

Nothing is more valuable and enjoyable than good conversation with other interesting people. Good conversation is hard to find. So, when you find one you must make a good impression and cooperate. That is, avoid letting your ego take the rein of your tongue. The big mistake many people make is that they try to impress the other person by showing how clever they are and do not really listen to them. This is like trying to take on the whole team and not passing the ball to a player who would have an easy tap-in.

The people in which the ego is dominant are self-absorbed and insecure. That is why they must prove they are special or intelligent. They do this not only to prove it to others, but also to themselves. If you are adept at doing something, have made an important contribution or have something important to say, then do so in a deliberate and empathetic manner. If you really are that good, then you have nothing to prove. A self-assured person does not have a needy ego and knows when, and when not to, try something special or to express their skill.

In whatever situation you find yourself, become aware of the influence of your ego and try to learn when to express your skill and when to give others the opportunity to show what they can do.

17

WE IMITATE POWERFUL PEOPLE

CRISTIANO RONALDO AND Messi are role models. A role model is an example, and an example is a person who we think is worthy of imitation. We would like to be like them.

There are two sides to the player we imitate. There is the professional side and the personal side. The professional side relates to the way someone like Ronaldo plays football. We imitate his stepover, dribbling and the way he strikes the ball. We might even imitate his attitude on the pitch. If we really admire him and he tends to be very aggressive and throws himself into a challenge, we are likely to do the same.

The personal life of a football celebrity is another source of influence on the fans. So, parents and members of society are very interested in what footballers do. When someone like John Terry cheats on his wife or Wayne Rooney is caught having sex with prostitutes, society is critical of their behaviour. We are critical because their fans, particularly the young ones, have a strong tendency to imitate them. This is because they admire them and even worship them. Young and impressionable fans tend to think: 'If Rooney does it, so should I', or, 'If I really want to be like Rooney, then I should have sex with prostitutes, too.'

Players like Rooney will protest that they do not make their fans do anything. It is true that Rooney does not grab his fan by the hand, drag him to a prostitute and wait until he has followed in Rooney's footsteps. Yet, Rooney, and other football stars, have an indirect power. They have the power to influence the actions of their fans.

Imitation is a subconscious activity. A fan of Rooney usually does not think, 'I'm going to imitate Rooney because I love him', and then proceed to do so. They simply imitate Rooney because human nature is structured in such a way that people tend to imitate those they admire and who are powerful. Football stars are worshipped, and their fans experience joy when they score a goal or execute a piece displaying brilliant skill. Stars of the game are paid many millions of dollars to play football, they live lives of luxury and are obsessively monitored by the media. Many people would like to live the life of a football star. Subconsciously, fans imitate the stars of the game because they hope to achieve or be associated with glory, respect, attention and the glamourous lifestyle.

The human tendency to imitate operates in our everyday interactions with other people. A guy I used to know was quick-witted. He would make a joke and everyone would burst out laughing. There was a moment when he was being witty and I felt myself wanting to make a joke too. As I did so, I recognised that I was imitating him, so I stopped myself. I did this because I was allowing my friend to influence me in a way that was incongruent with my own character and values. I'm not against making jokes and being the centre of attention, but it is out of character for me. It was unacceptable to me that he was indirectly influencing my subconscious mind.

The role model doesn't have to be a celebrity. It can be someone who has power, status or authority, be it parents, friends or a senior member of an organisation. All of us are influenced by other people, some more so than others. Becoming aware of the influence on us of others who we love, respect or admire empowers us to have some control over their influence. Most people don't realise they are imitating others because they do it subconsciously. Young people are particularly vulnerable because usually they have not developed their rational minds sufficiently or the tendency to reflect on their behaviour and ask themselves why they do what they do.

Intelligent people are also susceptible to the influence of famous or powerful people. In law school, a friend of mine appealed to Paris Hilton as an authority on social norms. She said, because Paris Hilton dresses her dog in clothes, it is okay to dress her dog in clothes too. I have nothing against Paris and I'm indifferent to whether a person puts clothes on their dog. What I find interesting is that an intelligent and educated person appealed to a celebrity to justify dressing up a dog.

Human beings will always imitate, and they imitate those who have power. This explains why people want to be lawyers, politicians, intellectuals, movie stars or football stars. They have power. Humans want power. Because humans want to possess and be associated with power, they imitate people they subconsciously judge are powerful. Being aware of this can help us to defend ourselves against the influence of other people, but it can also lead to greater self-knowledge and self-control.

PART FOUR
PRACTICAL WISDOM

SOCRATES, THE GRANDFATHER of modern Western philosophy, taught that when we know better we do better. We make mistakes only because we are ignorant of what we should do to act well. It is madness to want to improve ourselves without changing what we do, and what we do depends on what we think or understand we should do. If we learn a better way to do something and practice it, we will improve our game and ourselves. The attainment of wisdom, that is, knowledge of how to live and do well, is essential to becoming a better footballer or a master player in the game of life.

PART FOUR

PRACTICAL WISDOM

18

KNOWLEDGE IS POWER

KNOWLEDGE IS INDISPENSABLE to playing football successfully. We need knowledge of the rules. If you don't understand the offside rule, you are likely to be repeatedly caught offside and have a free kick awarded against you, or you will keep the opposition onside and indirectly help your opponents to score a goal. There are rules about what constitutes a correct throw-in, when the goalkeeper can handle the ball, what is an appropriate tackle, and what will be deemed a time-wasting activity. Acting in accord with a correct understanding of the rules ensures that you assist your team to win a football match.

Knowledge of the rules of football is power. It provides you with the ability to do more than you would if you lacked knowledge. Understanding the offside rule provides you with the ability to stay onside and avoid getting caught offside. This is obvious to experienced players, but players new to football often have trouble understanding the rule. They unwittingly get caught offside and give away a free kick.

Knowledge of strategy and skills empowers you to perform well on the pitch. Knowing how to put the right weight on a pass, when to pass, how to shield the ball, how to defend, when to push up, when to take on a player or take a shot, and that you must go to the ball when it is passed to you are principles essential to success. For instance, if you don't know how to put enough weight on the pass, then it is likely to be too short, and therefore likely to be intercepted by an opposing player. If it is too long, you are likely to give up possession to the opposition. Ignorance renders you ineffective, and often useless, whereas knowledge makes you more effective and provides you with the power to make something constructive happen, like creating an opportunity to score a goal.

There is another kind of knowledge that impacts your ability to play football. This is self-knowledge. Knowing what motivates you to play, why you make mistakes, why you are afraid to take risks, and why it is hard to be confident are useful things to know about yourself.

Personal insight assists you to identify mental and physical problems. This gives you the power to do something about these problems, which in turn has the capacity to increase your power to play football. If you are aware that you are missing your shots because you fear missing the target, then you are aware of the chief cause of your missed goals. Once you are aware of this cause, a piece of self-knowledge, you can use it to remedy the problem. For example, rather than imagining you will miss, focus only on kicking the ball with the correct technique. Application of this knowledge increases your power to score goals.

Without knowledge, you are impotent to do anything successfully in the game of football. Not only will you be incapable of positively contributing to the success of your team, you will be a burden. Your mistakes and lack of effective action are a source of weakness in the team. Your errors or unsuccessful actions put your team at risk of conceding goals, making it harder for your team to play cohesively and increase the risk of losing the game. Whereas, if you had perfect knowledge of all aspects of the game, the physics of the human body and the movement of the ball, knowledge of the general habits of defenders, strikers, and midfielders, the quirks of individual players, and knew how to perform all the tricks and skills, you would be unstoppable if you applied this knowledge.

This kind of extensive knowledge is an ideal or a description of the perfect footballer. No one has reached this ideal, but a few have got much closer than the rest of us. The key point is that the more knowledge you have of the various aspects of football, the more empowered you will be to affect a game. Being aware of the ideal gives us something to strive towards, knowing that, although we can never reach it, our continual acquisition of knowledge, experience and skill ensures that our footballing power is continually increasing.

It is easy to show that in life knowledge is power. Knowledge of the human body has led to medical treatments that have cured or controlled many illnesses and diseases. Knowledge of the atmosphere enables us to predict the weather, which empowers us to prepare our day in advance. Knowledge of logic and science led to the creation of computer technology, which enables us to instantly access information about almost anything that is known to humankind. Knowledge of the law enables us to defend our rights and organise our lives cohesively. Knowledge of physics enabled Einstein to explain how to harness atomic power. This might be the best proof for the claim that knowledge is power. The atomic bombs dropped on Japan in World War II showed the devastating power of atomic energy.

My favourite example is Tilly Smith, a 10-year-old girl on holidays in Thailand in 2004 with her family. While walking along the beach with her parents, Tilly noticed the sea behaving strangely. It was foamy, agitated and continuously coming in, rather than coming in and then going back out again. The behaviour of the sea matched what she had recently learned at school about tsunamis. She quickly realised that a tsunami was coming.

She explained this to her parents, who did not possess knowledge of tsunamis. Tilly's parents told her she was mistaken, that there was nothing to worry about and continued walking along the beach. Her understanding, however, made her imagine the dreadful consequences of not vacating the beach immediately. She became panic-stricken and demanded that her parents take their family away from the beach. She dropped to the sand and said she knew what was going to happen. She said there was going to be a giant wave. This unsettled her father and caused her sister to cry uncontrollably. Tilley's father took her younger sister back to the hotel, but her mother kept on walking. Tilly pleaded with her mother to go back to the hotel, but she would not listen to her. Reluctantly, Tilly left her mother on the beach and ran back to the hotel.

There, Tilly's father told a Japanese security guard what his daughter had said about the tsunami. Fortunately, he knew the word *tsunami* (it is a Japanese word) and had earlier learned that there had been an enormous earthquake in Sumatra and that a tsunami might occur. This was enough for the security guard to evacuate the beach. Not long after, the tsunami came rolling in, engulfing the beach and smashing everything in its path. Tilly had the power to help save many lives that day because of her *knowledge* of tsunamis. This story teaches us that knowledge can empower people of almost any age.

Rarely will we need this kind of knowledge and power in our everyday lives. I used to think that the most useful kind of knowledge is knowledge of the law. The law governs almost every aspect of our lives. I reasoned that if I knew the law well, then I would be able to use the law to defend my rights, defend the rights of others, and to contribute to the construction of better laws to help improve the organisation of society and the way in which it is governed. That is why I studied the law.

I still think that knowledge of the law is valuable. Now, I believe that the two best types of knowledge one could possess are knowledge of how to communicate well with others and knowledge of human nature. The value of the latter is a presupposition of the book, which is demonstrated in several chapters (for example, Chapters 20 and 22). Here, I will use examples to illustrate the value of the former.

I have visited China with my Chinese wife several times: two experiences stand out. First, whenever my wife left me alone, I would feel anxious. This was because most Chinese people cannot speak English well. So, if I was separated from her, I could not communicate anything about myself, my wife, the hotel I was staying at and so on. The second example was on a repeat visit to China. My wife explained to me how to ask for a large coffee in Chinese. I did so, and the assistant nodded and punched in the order, but then he spoke to me in Chinese. I had no idea what he was saying, so I called over my wife to translate. Her translation was: 'Having the coffee here or taking it away?'

My inability to speak Chinese made me powerless and vulnerable. Clearly, if I could have spoken Chinese in the above situations I would have been powerful and self-reliant. This shows that knowing how to communicate well is a source of power. Being able to articulate your thoughts to another person enables you to get what you want, persuade another person to cooperate with you or to bond with other people.

What about when you must communicate with a loved one, your manager or an authority figure, something that may involve strong emotions? In this kind of situation, it is crucial that you communicate your thoughts precisely and try to understand what the other person is saying to you. This reminds me of Emerson's observation that children's tantrums are an expression of the frustration of their desires, but once they can communicate their desires, they are less prone to throwing a tantrum.

This insight can be extended to adolescents and adults. There are people of all ages who lack the ability to articulate their thoughts. This deficiency causes frustration in themselves and others and can lead to anger and its consequences. Since everyone's ability to communicate is at a different stage of development for various reasons, it is easy to see why there is so much miscommunication or simply a lack of good communication. This observation should encourage us to be tolerant of others and to try to understand rather than judge them.

The best communicators usually have powerful positions in society. Presidents, prime ministers, CEOs, professors, business people, lawyers, doctors and psychologists are highly skilled communicators. Even in football, the most powerful tend to be good communicators. The coach must be a good communicator for the players to apply their strategy or tactics effectively. The captain must be a good communicator for their teammates to follow them. However, the skilful use of vocabulary is not always necessary, particularly in the case of a captain or a leader. As the author Jim Rohn recognised, all Jesus had to say was 'follow me'.

This is evident in football, too. Captains have experience, toughness and skill, so when they say, 'follow me' or 'do x', their teammates do it, mostly because of all that they are as footballers. Liverpool's former captain Steven Gerrard is an excellent example. His tenacity, miraculous goals, unparalleled stamina and determination inspired his teammates to get the best out of themselves.

Many philosophers have emphasised that knowledge is power, such as Francis Bacon, Spinoza, Emerson and Friedrich Nietzsche. Knowledge of science, human nature, your own nature and the tendencies of others can empower you. If you want to enhance your results in football or some other area of life, increasing your knowledge of relevant laws (natural or human made), strategies, conventions and habits is one of the most useful things you can do. Next time you are inspired by a footballer's genius, a great speech or some person's superior ability, remember that they can do it because they have empowered themselves through the acquisition of knowledge, and that their application of knowledge is what inspires you.

19

ALL HUMAN CREATIONS AND ACHIEVEMENTS CAN BE TRACED TO IDEAS

SOME PEOPLE THINK ideas are impractical. We might argue that ideas can't help you win a football match or kick a goal for you. This objection can be met by explaining what an idea is and its relation to what we do. An idea is a kind of belief that explains the world or part of it, or provides instructions on how to realise something in the world.

Football itself is an idea. Football is the belief that there is a game in which there are two goals at opposite ends of a patch of grass, there are eleven players on each side, both teams have a goalkeeper and the aim of the game is for each team to get a spherical ball completely across their opponent's goal line. This idea or belief makes the game of football possible. What this shows is that an *idea* gave rise to the beautiful game.

Ideas are needed to play football well and successfully. Imagine playing with no ideas except a rudimentary idea of football. That is, the aim of football is to get the ball across the goal line. You would probably run wherever the ball was and swing your foot at the ball haphazardly whenever it came near you. Without the ideas of position, making space, marking your player and keeping goal side, you would be hopeless. But, it would be by acting in accordance with the ideas of holding your position, making space and keeping goal side of your opponent that would enable you to play the game effectively. Moreover, acting in accordance with correct ideas helps you to play well, whereas incorrect ideas lead to unfavourable results.

Many ideas in life are not about real things, but we treat them as though they are. We must learn to distinguish ideas of real things, things that can't be changed, from those that are fictions. For example, the idea that living human beings play the game of football is real, for when you watch a live football match that is exactly what you see. But, the idea of a penalty is not of a thing that exists independently of the human mind. It is an *idea* or a belief that because a player has been fouled inside the 18-yard box, they should have a free kick at the goalkeeper.

The first or real idea cannot be changed, that is, the idea of an existing human being, but the idea of a penalty can. If we thought that the idea of a penalty should be removed from the game, we could do that. What is important is that we act in accordance with these ideas. If a player is fouled inside the opposition's 18-yard box, which is part of the idea of a penalty, we give them a free kick at the goalkeeper. The *application* of ideas has real consequences.

This applies to most areas of life. There are many ideas that are fictions. For example, Australia is understood to be a real thing, a country that exists in the world. Australia is a fiction. The idea of Australia refers to a certain piece of land that exists in a certain part of the world. There are human beings who live there. These ideas are true. But, most other descriptors of Australia are likely to be fictions. Australia is a liberal representative democracy. The values of Australia include 'a fair go' and multiculturalism. The 'typical' Aussie likes footy and 'a snag on the barbie'. These ideas are fictions in that you will not find the things existing independently of human beings and their actions.

Nonetheless, as in football, these ideas, though fictional, have real consequences. The idea of multiculturalism is used to guide people's behaviour in Australia; for example, the kinds of things that are taught to children, foreign and domestic policy, and the types of articles that can be non-controversially written on social media. However, since they are simply ideas, they can be changed.

When I was an adolescent, I used to think doctors and lawyers were special people. They were foreign to me and I believed that I was fundamentally different from them. My time in university led me to realise that doctors, lawyers and other professionals, as well as celebrities and football stars, are not special at all. They are merely human beings just like me and everyone else on the planet. That is not to say that the nature of their work is not important or that they have not worked hard to become, say, a doctor or lawyer.

It just means that because my ideas of them have changed, so too have my perception and feelings about them. I no longer feel intimidated, inferior or in awe of doctors, lawyers, professors or anyone because of their status in life. This shows that, if we change our ideas of things, be they related to our perceptions of others or areas such as the law, the application of ideas has the power to change how we see, feel and act.

One day in law school, while reading a piece of legislation, it occurred to me that the law is nothing but words and ideas. The force of the law comes from *human beings* making you do things in accordance with the words and ideas that are labelled 'laws'. But, since the law consists only of words and ideas, it follows that the law is not fixed. Yet, the law, when it is applied, has real consequences. Before the late 20th Century, a husband forcing his wife to have sex with him was not guilty of rape because of the ideas that made up the law at that time. In countries like Australia, the ideas that constitute the law relating to rape have changed, so that a husband can now be found guilty of raping his wife, if his actions fit the definition or idea of rape.

Ideas have practical value. We act in accordance with ideas all the time. Some ideas are real and some are fictions. The latter are changeable. However, ideas, or the actions that follow them, have real consequences. If we want good consequences, to win the football match or to play well, to find the ideal partner, the job of our dreams or to create a fairer and happier world, we must make sure we have good ideas guiding our actions.

20

UNDERSTANDING ENABLES US TO APPRECIATE THE GAME

SOME PEOPLE THINK football is boring. They find it hard to understand why millions of people enjoy watching grown men or women kick a ball around on the park just to get the ball across a line between two goal posts. Why do some people love football and others dislike it? Football itself doesn't make one person love it and another hate, or be indifferent to, it. The reason for the love, hate or indifference is the psychology of the individual person.

A key difference between the lovers and the haters is that the lovers usually know the rules of the game and the skills or knowledge one needs to play football successfully. The enthusiast, someone who has played, or followed, the game for a long time, tends to appreciate football when it is played well. Playing the offside rule effectively, a player holding the ball up to allow teammates to regroup or push forward, or executing a formation or drill well provides one who understands the game with much joy. Being able to understand the complexity and difficulty of performing football skills correctly enables the enthusiast to perceive the value of football.

There are many people who think life is pointless and contains nothing of value. From a certain perspective, this kind of thinking seems reasonable. How can you appreciate life when there is so much suffering, frustration, disappointment, confusion, and conflict? I've met many people who have expressed these sorts of feelings and thoughts to me. It's not hard to understand why they think and feel that way.

Look around and you will see people all in a fuss trying to get to some place that they probably won't really like when they get there. In modern societies in countries like Australia, the US and the UK, people are expected to work most of the day and then make time for family and friends. If they are particularly responsible citizens, they should be politically and socially active, and then somehow find time for themselves.

Innumerable desires are frustrated, people let you down, and there is conflict between family members, neighbours and nations. We are given contradictory advice, for example, milk is good for you and milk is bad for you. Many of us seek advice about how to be happy, and there are others who are determined to destroy the *myth* of happiness. This kind of bewildered thinking is like the apathetic spectator who only sees the ball bouncing off this person's head, that person's foot striking the ball and the ball hitting the back of the net. The spectator asks, 'What's the point?' All this sweating and heavy breathing just to get the ball from one side of the pitch to the other seems like a meaningless waste of time. Similarly, it seems to the unenthusiastic spectator of life that there is a lot of sweating, heavy breathing and red cheeks, which seem just as meaningless.

The negative aspects discussed above are usually not an issue for people who understand the principles of life. Life does not puzzle life enthusiasts. Like their football counterparts, life enthusiasts know the rules of the game they are playing. For this reason, both kinds of enthusiast appreciate the games they watch and play.

Knowing the laws of life can be a source of joy. According to Spinoza, the greatest happiness for a human being is to understand nature and its laws. He also said that understanding the laws of human nature, particularly the causes and laws of the emotions, can be a rich source of enjoyment. Einstein, who admired Spinoza, agreed with him. Einstein said he wanted to know the mind of God, which he identified with the laws of nature that govern the whole universe. Contemplation of the universal laws of nature filled Einstein with joy.

A fundamental law of nature is that a body continues in a state of rest or a fixed rate of motion in a straight line unless an external force changes its state. This is the principle of inertia or Newton's first law of motion. Spinoza considers this a fundamental law of nature. Spinoza differs from most other thinkers in that he applies this principle to the nature of human beings and their actions. He explains that all things strive to preserve themselves. In relation to our bodies, the power by which we strive to preserve ourselves is the motion imparted to us by external causes, namely, the bodies of our parents. So, our bodies will continue in this state of motion, that is, we will continue to strive to preserve our bodies, unless an external force changes this state, namely, it destroys us. If there were no external causes more powerful than the power by which we strive to preserve ourselves, we would live forever.

We all know that there are infinite things more powerful than human beings. Yet, the power by which we strive to preserve ourselves is part of the power of nature. The power of the things that can destroy us arises from the same thing that created us. As Emerson says, 'Let us build altars to the Beautiful Necessity, which secures that all is made of one piece; that plaintiff and defendant, friend and enemy, animal and planet, food and eater, are of one kind.' And Emerson asks, 'Why should we be afraid of Nature, which is no other than "philosophy and theology embodied"? Why should we fear to be crushed by savage elements, we who are made up of the same elements?' As I will explain below, Emerson, like Einstein and Spinoza, believes that divine power permeates nature or the universe.

Everything comes from this divine power. So, we should not be afraid of nature and its laws. We should try to understand and use them.

Spinoza's derivation of the principle of inertia is a familiar law of life. Most of us have learned the principle of self-preservation from experience. What makes Spinoza interesting is that he explains why this is an inherent property of the universe. Guiding our thoughts by this principle can help us to make sense of what we and others do, which can make our experience of life more interesting and enjoyable and may even reduce our anxiety. For example, where there are two lanes close together with vehicles travelling in opposite directions, you might fear that a car heading towards you will veer into your lane and crash into your car. Application of the above rule of life will lessen or remove your anxiety because you will understand that nearly everyone must stay in their own lane because they strive to preserve themselves, like everyone else.

A conversation with a friend provides another example. My friend was very interested in a girl he had met. He had made his interest known to her, but he complained that she was holding back. I explained to him that she fears rejection, which is a specific application of the instinct to self-preservation, just as much as he does. This insight changed his perception of the situation and made him tolerant and patient in his pursuit of the girl he liked. What the above examples show is that the more you understand the laws of human nature and emotions, the less stress you are likely to suffer and the richer your experience of ordinary life.

Even if you want an ultimate purpose to make life meaningful for you, this principle still applies. If you believe in a god, then you should recognise that this god made the laws that govern the universe and human nature. By understanding the laws, you can come to have a better understanding and appreciation of this god's handiwork.

There are alternative approaches, of course. Spinoza, Emerson, Einstein and the Stoics recognised the divinity within nature. Their respective views of this divine element vary greatly. But, in general, one can hold that only nature exists and that there is no god above the natural world that created it. And that, by understanding the laws, you understand the thing that created you, nature itself.

Understanding the laws of the universe and your own nature leads to self-knowledge. Rather than wandering through life with a puzzled look on your face and perceiving things to be random and meaningless, you will instead increasingly understand (as you continually increase your knowledge of the principles of nature) why people do what they do and perceive the divine intelligence that exists within yourself and the rest of the world. By increasing your knowledge of the laws of life you will increase your capacity to appreciate the game and live more joyfully.

21

THE MORE YOU CAN DO AND THE BETTER YOU UNDERSTAND THE GAME, THE MORE YOU WILL ENJOY IT

PLAYERS WHO ARE ignorant of the rules of football and lack ability will have a bad experience of the game. They are unlikely to get the ball because they don't know how to make space for themselves. They will be prone to losing the ball when it arrives at their feet because they don't know how to control it. It will be difficult for them to help their team retain possession of the ball because they haven't developed good passing technique. Since there will be little or no joy for them, they'll probably want to give up and move to the sidelines.

The same is true of players in the game of life. If you don't know the rules or how to play, life will be an unhappy experience. The ball represents opportunity. If you don't know the rules or how to play, then you are unlikely to get an opportunity or to take it. Of course, as in football, the ball might roll to you fortuitously, so an opportunity might come your way without any effort on your part. Without the relevant skills, however, you are likely to waste the opportunity. Life is tough for a player who is ignorant of the rules of life and lacks life skills. So, if you want the 'ball' or to score a goal, you must learn the rules and develop your skills.

This principle can be applied to almost any human activity. If you know what to do, not only are you more likely to get what you want, but applying your knowledge will be enjoyable. Spinoza and Emerson observed that joy expresses true power. Emerson said, 'power dwells with cheerfulness; hope puts us in a working mood, whilst despair is no muse, and untunes the active powers.' According to Spinoza, joy is an emotion by which a human being transitions to a greater state of power. So, the more joy we experience, the more powerful we must be.

When you know what to do in football, you don't worry about making a mistake. Instead, you focus on the correct performance of your skills. The correct execution of skill has two benefits. Joy accompanies ability, so when we perform our skills well, we necessarily experience joy. That's why Ronaldinho played with a smile on his face. The other benefit is that our passes and shots on goal tend to be on target, which increase our chances of our team scoring a goal and winning the match.

However, there is a huge difference between football and life. Unlike football, where you might decide to participate at any age, when you are five or fifty-five, you are forced into the game of life on the very first day you enter the world. During that time, other people, mainly your parents, play the game for you. Then you are supposed to be taught the rules and equipped with the skills of life. Some of us are lucky to have good guides from the beginning, whereas others are not so lucky.

There are rules and skills that almost everyone learns. Then again, there are rules and skills that many don't learn because they don't have someone to exemplify them or encourage their acquisition. The ability to communicate is common, but many people are not skilful communicators. Most of us learn this skill subconsciously and reactively, but few do so consciously and proactively. Articulate people tend to be successful in life. This indicates that an underdeveloped ability to communicate is an enormous disadvantage. It is difficult to maintain relationships of any kind without good communication skills.

Life is less enjoyable for those lacking skill, knowledge and ability. While some people have holidays overseas because they know how to book a flight, a hotel and get to their destination, others stay at home in front of the television or go online. They do this, not necessarily because they don't want to go on a fun trip, but because the thought of really going on an overseas holiday makes them anxious, which arises because they lack the ability to plan it. Hence, they believe they can't organise an overseas trip. Their belief creates their reality. For the people whose life skills are unripe, their journey through life is unnecessarily devoid of the best kinds of experiences.

If you hate or are anxious about life, it may be because you haven't adequately developed your life skills and learned the rules that govern it. You may have developed your skills to some extent, but perhaps not to a high degree. If this describes your situation, then there is hope for you. It's possible for you to understand the game, learn the rules and develop your life skills. You can love playing the game of life as much as Ronaldinho loved to play football.

In football and life, if we lack understanding or the ability to influence the game, we feel confused and useless. Consequently, we experience sadness. The solution is to increase our understanding of the game and develop our skills. By doing so, we will increase our power to play the game well, which must be accompanied by joy and cheerfulness. The masters of the game of life, for example, Spinoza, Emerson and Einstein, were known for their cheerful dispositions. Even though Einstein was an imperfect human being, made mistakes and experienced sadness on many occasions, he was a master of life. That Einstein was a cheerful person is unsurprising and this can be attributed to his wisdom.

22

A WISE PLAYER LOOKS UP

A FUNDAMENTAL RULE of football is that you should look up when you have the ball at your feet. You need to do this so you can see in what direction you are heading and where your opponents and teammates are, while controlling the ball. This is crucial to help you become aware of your options and it gives you more freedom to decide what to do with the ball. A player who looks only at the ball is likely to run straight into trouble.

If you are a beginner, you must get used to looking up when you have the ball at your feet. This takes time and practice. The more you do it the more you will be able to sense and feel where the ball is. The more experience you have looking up when you have the ball at your feet, the more natural it will feel. You will just *know* where it is. Then you will be able to take your eyes away from the ball and use them to decide what to do with it.

Pat Nevin was a Scottish footballer who successfully incorporated this principle into his own game. Nevin played for Chelsea, Everton and several other clubs. He was recognised as a skilful dribbler of the ball. He attributes his ability to dribble the ball past defenders to his one-on-one sessions with his Dad. Nevin would wait for his father to come home from work to practice dribbling the ball. He would repeatedly dribble the ball in and out of cones, alternating his weaker and stronger feet, and with his eyes closed. By the age of nine he did not have to look at the ball because he knew where it was and he could feel it.

Imagine a child's parents adopted the same approach as Nevin's father in relation to general life skills. Every day one of the child's parents would do one-on-one sessions in which the child would practice the skills of communication and reflective thinking. By the time the child reached adulthood, he or she would not only be a highly skilled communicator and thinker, but also an independent and self-assured human being. Rather than looking down and hoping life would turn out well, a child who had this kind of preparation would look up and face life head-on. A person who had this kind of upbringing would know they could speak and act well spontaneously and self-assuredly, just as Nevin could dribble the ball without looking at it.

Developing your ability to think and filling your mind with good ideas and knowledge is equivalent to looking up in football, for thinking and knowledge enlarge your field of perception. Knowledge of the laws of physical nature enable us to see what others cannot see. Tilly Smith's understanding of the nature of tsunamis gave her a clear perception of an imminent tsunami, while her parents who lacked this knowledge were oblivious to its existence (discussed in Chapter 18).

People who understand can perceive motives, intentions and feelings that people ignorant of body language cannot. A person knowledgeable about body language can tell by the direction and movement of a person's feet whether they like another individual or not. Similarly, knowledge of the principles of human nature enable us to perceive people's true motivations, whereas uninformed people are blind to them.

Alan Penn, a Professor in Architectural and Urban Computing, explains the motivation for the store lay out of a certain giant furniture retailer. IKEA's design of a set path through its stores and its organisation of its shelves obliges shoppers to see as many of its products as possible. There are short cuts, but they are difficult to find. IKEA hopes that the lay out will tempt shoppers to purchase more products than they intended. Company representatives might deny this, but their economic self-interest, which is a manifestation of their nature to preserve themselves, determines that it must be true.

Most supermarkets and department stores use similar tactics to influence the behaviour of their customers. Likewise, marketers and salespeople use a range of tricks to try to influence people to purchase their products or services. This insight should not stop us from, say, shopping at IKEA. It can help us to focus only on what we intended to buy and to not be distracted by the other products that are strategically presented to us. This awareness will keep our pockets fuller than they might otherwise have been and make us less susceptible to psychological manipulation.

You might wonder why it can be hard for a player to look up or become more aware of their surroundings. We keep our eyes on the ball because we do not feel in control of it and we fear losing possession. This is analogous to many areas of life. For example, we continuously talk because we don't feel in control of ourselves, we feel inadequate or we fear that we will be rejected.

In football, no one can be fully in control because the ball is almost always moving and so are the other players on the pitch, which means you can't focus on only one aspect of what you are doing. Similarly, conversation is a dynamic activity that often takes unexpected turns. To be able to remain active and in control of your participation in the conversation, you need to listen to the other person, consider what they are saying and then think about what you want to reply or do. It's the difference between being self-conscious and other-conscious, or looking at the ball and *looking up*.

23

COMMUNICATION IS THE MOST FUNDAMENTAL HUMAN SKILL

THERE ARE MANY skills in football. The most important skill is the ability to communicate with your teammates. Communication can be verbal or nonverbal. You might say to a teammate, 'time', 'you're hot', 'through ball' or 'switch'. You might also give a teammate a certain look or nod, or dart one way to throw your opponent off and then race in the opposite direction. Your teammates understand these acts of communication because of practice drills and experience playing with you.

Good communication usually leads to goals and winning football matches, whereas poor communication leads to conceding goals and losing matches. This is the glue that makes a champion team function well, yet the glue is often weak, low quality or even absent in a team because of each individual star's own vainglory. An obvious example is an open player in attack. The player with the ball might say, 'give me something'. The glory-seeker, however, might only pretend to be interested in what their teammates are doing and intend to take a shot no matter how advantageous their teammates' positions.

An unsighted player with the ball might hear a teammate shout 'I'm open' (say this teammate is near the penalty spot and the player with the ball is out wide and in line with them). Now, if the open player says nothing, the blinded player in possession of the ball will probably assume that they are alone and so will shoot for goal, but if they hear the call from the teammate, the player will have the opportunity to set up an easy goal. Unselfish players try to get the ball to the open player and greedy players ignore their teammate and take the shot, even if it is impossible to score.

The key factor that would lead to a goal in this case is communication, not the position of the open player or the thinking of the player in possession of the ball. In this situation, the selfish player will not score. It happens often at all levels and in most team sports. Without communication, the player in possession would be unaware of their teammate, so communication is vital to scoring the goal.

There are skills needed to flourish in life. As in football, the most important skill is the ability to communicate. In football, if you cannot communicate to your teammate where you want the ball, they are unlikely to put the ball where you want it, unless it gets there by luck. Likewise, if you do not communicate what you want from a person in a personal or professional relationship, they will not know what to do to make you happy. The upshot is that you are likely to be frustrated or disappointed.

Your body language is part of what is communicated to other people. As Emerson says, 'What you *are* stands over you the while and thunders so that I cannot hear what you say to the contrary.' Emerson's point is that your body language is more persuasive than your words. You might tell a teammate you think they are a good player, but that you never pass the ball to them shows that you really think they are not a good player. Your teammate will grow deaf to your words about their ability and instead will pay attention to what you do.

Your words and what you do together constitute a mode of communication that others perceive and interpret. Being a good communicator and collaborator requires more than articulacy; it also requires sincerity, specifically in the form of behaving in accordance with your words. Your actions must communicate the same message as your words if you want people to trust you and cooperate with you.

Good communication does not guarantee success or compliance with your wishes. Without good communication, however, the ball is unlikely to come to you. Your children, your partner, colleagues or friends are far less likely to do what you want or assist you. But, if you are a good communicator, then people will be attracted to you, want to converse with you, work with you and help you.

24

SIMPLICITY IS SUPERIOR TO COMPLEXITY

MOST OF US want to shine when we play football. The desire to produce the spectacular inspires people to be creative and it motivates them to do their best. The problem is that some players are determined to do something extraordinary every time they get the ball. Beating one or even two players isn't enough. They must beat the whole team or, having beaten a player, they decide to try to beat that player again. 'Superstars' regularly take shots from impossible angles or from too far out. Their ego wants them to stand out, but the problem is that usually their ego lets the team down.

A player's ego is opposed to the team and it is the cause of the extravagant and overambitious attempts in football. Instead of a simple pass to a teammate, the egotistical player tries to beat an opponent or do an impressive flick. What amateurs tend not to understand is that professionals *usually* make the simple pass instead of the fancy one. The opposite seems to be the case in non-professional games. Undeniably, professionals have egos, too, and on occasion they try a backheel that fails when a simple pass would have been best.

A failed fancy action is bad because it often leads to dispossession. It can increase team disharmony. Your teammates are likely to be angry with you for not making the simple pass. Simplicity, in the sense of performing a basic skill well, is more likely to reach its target. The benefits of simplicity are that it's less likely to result in your teammates having negative feelings associated with you and punishment in terms of loss of ground or concession of a goal.

In everyday life, there are many examples of people taking the more complex approach rather than keeping it simple. Usually, the ego is behind this. There is another motive, though. This is the desire to sell you stuff. Salespeople appeal to the ego, the need to feel in control or the desire to obtain something with minimal effort. A good example is health and fitness. The innumerable diets, health books, programs and machines on the market make it hard to discover what really will improve health and fitness.

The principles of health, fitness and strength are simple and have been known for thousands of years. They're based on common sense. For the health of the body, eat moderate amounts of fruit, vegetables and meat and do so only when you are hungry. For fitness, be physically active, for instance, go walking, running, riding or play a sport for an hour or two every day. For strength, do push-ups, sit-ups, dips, chin-ups and other compound weight-lifting exercises regularly, always pushing yourself and adding weight or repetitions once it becomes too easy. Do all of this and you will be fit, healthy and strong.

Every health or fitness book will mention in some way these things. So that the book appears authoritative, it will use jargon, refer to research that is full of technicalities and statistics, or to some expert. Of course, they will emphasise some secret to health, fitness or strength that is the reason for the existence of the book. Yet, the book will include the basics referred to above. It is better to ignore the technicalities and appeal to research. Stick to what is simple and what works, that is, common sense.

If it is so simple, why do so many people struggle to be fit, healthy and strong? The main reason is modern life. Cars have replaced walking. Fast food restaurants, instant meals and home-delivery foods have replaced hunting. The television and the Internet have replaced social activities like dancing. These days people exert as little energy as possible and try to maximise sensual pleasure.

There are many obstacles to living a simple life. Having to work forty hours plus per week, taking care of our kids, and the numerous other responsibilities that demand our attention and time often undermine our attempts to keep ourselves healthy, fit and strong, so we shouldn't be too hard on ourselves when we do not get the results we want. However, we should always try to keep our approach to health and fitness, or any other area of life, as simple as possible.

By keeping it simple, you focus on achieving real positive results. By contrast, the unnecessary complication of an activity indicates that you care too much about how you are perceived by other people. This kind of behaviour reflects a needy ego, whereas a person who sticks to the fundamentals is wise and self-assured. Whatever area of your life you want to improve, be it your education, profession, business, parenting or football, avoid those who needlessly complicate the activity and concentrate on the fundamentals.

25

RUSHING INVITES ERROR

ONE OF THE worst things a footballer can do is rush a pass, tackle or shot on goal. Rushing can be the difference between a goal being scored or not, and defeat or victory. On the other hand, sometimes we need to deal with the ball quickly. There is a difference between rushing and first-time plays, though. Rushing a pass can be disastrous, whereas a first-time pass is often the key to penetrating a dogged defence. Absent from a rushed pass is prior thinking, however brief, before it was executed. In a first-time play, you pass or shoot the ball as soon as it comes to you, but you do so in a controlled and deliberate manner. By contrast, the rushed play usually involves a lack of control and focus.

It is very important to take your time in football. When you rush a pass or shot on goal, the chances of you making a mistake rise considerably. This is because concentration is needed to correctly execute your skills. Rather than hitting the ball in its middle, you swipe at it and the ball goes flying off the side of your boot.

There are several causes of rushing a play. Misjudgement is one of them. A major cause is anxiety. You fear that you are going to make a mistake. This fear is connected to your subconscious awareness and interpretation of the stakes involved. As a result, you rush your pass or shot, and the ball ends up nowhere near where you hoped it would go.

Only self-assured players can take their time with the ball. Self-assurance springs from footballing ability. In football and life, there is no simple and quick fix to a low level of self-assurance. Time, study and work are necessary to the attainment of self-assurance and, therefore, the ability to take your time.

What you can do, however, is in every play where you have possession of the ball, remind yourself of this principle. Tell yourself that this is just one moment in a game and it will eventually be forgotten, even if it leads to concession of a goal or defeat. If rushing the play is likely to lead to error anyway, then taking your time to get it right, even though it is nearly as likely to lead to error, is not such a big risk to take. Rather, it will put you in the mindset of depending on yourself, focusing on executing your skills and taking control of the play.

The most rewarding consequence of this approach is that each time will result in another piece of experience and refinement of judgment and skill. In every play and game that you consciously do this, you will improve. Your persistence will result in self-assurance and the ability to take your time.

Taking your time is beneficial in virtually all areas of life. This is a principle of nature. It is to the advantage of all living things to be patient and take their time. The tiger must be patient when it stalks its prey. Watch a tiger cub learning to catch its prey. It will usually be too eager and give away its presence. Its prey easily gets away. No food for the tiger cub. Fortunately, the cub has its mother there to teach it. Eventually, the tiger cub grows and learns the vital importance of patience. It will watch and wait, and wait, and creep silently towards its victim, and wait, and wait, until it judges it is close enough to pounce before it is detected. The reward of patience for the tiger is food in the stomach and continued life.

Taking your time is crucial to making the most of the biggest events in your life. If you rush in for the kiss, you might put off your date and ruin a perfect night. If you take your time, you might be rewarded with the affection you crave. If you speak too quickly, people will find it hard to follow you and will probably misunderstand you, or you might say something regrettable.

Powerful people tend to talk slowly, while insecure people usually speak quickly. In football, it is the same. The most powerful players—that is, the most skilful and talented— take their time, whereas the weaker players—the least skilful and talented—tend to rush themselves. So, by increasing your power (skills, abilities, awareness and knowledge) you will be able to take your time when you perform an action, like selling your good points to a potential employer, wooing the girl or guy of your dreams, or executing your intention to put the ball in the back of the net. Remember, the tiger cub had to learn to be patient, that is, it acquired knowledge needed to catch its prey and to live. In football and life, patience manifests wisdom.

It is not always possible or desirable to take your time. Still, it is best to try to act deliberately, rather than without any direction, that is, to hit and hope. Our spontaneous words and actions can harm our relationships with our loved ones, our children and our colleagues. We need to develop our communication skills and our understanding of human nature so that we can feel sure that what we want to say or do will hit the mark. Self-assurance enables us to take our time and this increases the effectiveness of our actions and inspires confidence and trust in others.

26

EVEN THE BEST PLAYERS MISS MORE THAN THEY SCORE

IMAGINE CRISTIANO RONALDO or Messi missing a shot on goal. It does happen. The very best attacking players miss many more than they score. The great players do not give up after they have missed the goal, no matter how embarrassing it was. Even if they have just missed the target, the next time they get the ball in a goal-scoring position, they will shoot again.

Before 2018, Messi's record against Chelsea had been awful. In eight matches or 655 minutes, Messi was scoreless, despite taking twenty-nine shots on goal. He even failed to score against Chelsea in both legs of the 2011–12 Champions League semi-final, when he was at the height of his footballing powers, a season in which he scored seventy-three goals in sixty games, a European club record. In the round of 16 of the 2017–18 Champions League, Messi scored three times against Chelsea, but even those goals were due to luck and Chelsea errors more than his own creativity and skill. It is also worth noting that after his performances against Chelsea, Messi and Barcelona were knocked out by Roma in the quarter-finals. He did not score in either leg and his performance in the second leg was uninspired.

Messi is one of the greatest footballers to ever play the game. He has scored some of the most fantastic goals in the history of football. Nevertheless, even he performs poorly sometimes and makes mistakes. He is one of my favourite players, but this does not prevent me from perceiving his human foibles. It also helps me to be less critical of myself when I miss a shot on goal, and it encourages me to try again after I have missed a shot or made a mistake.

Here is a different kind of case study. While he was at Liverpool, Fernando Torres seemed to be an outstanding striker. Chelsea signed him for a record fee. The transfer seemed like good business for Chelsea and bad for their opponents. Surprisingly, Torres took 903 minutes to score his first goal and he subsequently continued to struggle to score goals for Chelsea. Torres was consequently ridiculed and his ability to score was doubted by many critics. His failure to score in front of an open goal against Manchester United in the 2011–12 season is one of the worst misses ever by a player. He never lived up to the hype at Chelsea, although he did score important goals for the club. Despite his misses, Torres never stopped trying to score a goal next time he was in front of the goal with the ball at his feet.

This principle applies to the goals in the other parts of your life. There are the goals of finding a girlfriend or boyfriend, securing a job you really want, winning the promotion or raising healthy and self-reliant children. Imagine you gave up trying to find a partner after your first try. What would be the consequence? A life of being single. You can be sure that everyone has missed this goal or been rejected at least once in their lives. Even the most attractive people are rejected. Still, those who successfully get the girl or guy are those who are willing to take a shot the next time the opportunity presents itself.

Life is full of opportunities. No matter what your goals are, if you put yourself in front of them, you might achieve them. Conversely, you might be very talented and skilful, but there will be times when you will squander your chances. Like Messi and Torres, you should keep trying. Forget the missed opportunity and put yourself in a position to have another chance. Accept that whether you score a goal is not entirely up to you, since luck must have its say. Never give up and you will score a goal sooner or later.

27

COURAGE IS FOCUSING ON DOING WHAT YOU MUST

WINNING POSSESSION OF the ball is everything. Without the ball, you cannot score a goal. If you cannot score a goal, you cannot win a football match. The virtue you must possess if you want to win the ball is courage. Emerson said, 'the high price of courage indicates the general timidity'. True courage is rare because most of us are unwilling to pay the price of the thing we want.

A part of courage is acting despite the feeling of fear. It means you compete for what you want, even though you feel afraid. Contesting the ball in the air, diving in for the tackle, and taking on an opponent are actions that demand courage.

Why do these actions cause fear? Fear is an expression of the body's perception of a threat to its wellbeing. We fear a clash of heads, an injury or being dispossessed of the ball. We want to avoid what we imagine will cause us pain. The image of a clash of heads, studs crashing into our shins or copping the ball in the groin makes us hesitate and want to avoid the encounter. We fear that if we lose the ball, we will have to exert a tremendous amount of energy to recover it, or worse, our mistake will be punished by the concession of a goal.

Ultimately, the instinct for self-preservation underlies our fears. We want to increase the advantage of the team, but we also want to preserve our bodies. Courage is expensive because you must risk your wellbeing *or* your power to preserve yourself to have the chance to win a play or a football match.

The secret to courage is focus. Focus is about what you desire most. It is the difference between the desire to win the ball and the desire to avoid injury or loss. The courageous person takes the risk of being elbowed in the face or dispossessed, but they focus on winning the contest. You will find that the most courageous people are the ones who care less about getting hurt and more about winning the ball and winning the game. Their desire to win the ball or game is so strong that the thought of getting hurt does not enter their mind or, if it does, it is only momentary. And, because cowardice is more common than courage, the courageous player usually wins possession of the ball.

One way to build up your courage and overcome your fear is to force yourself to make the challenge or take the risk. If you focus on winning the ball fairly and not recklessly, but with skill and good judgment, then three positive consequences will follow. You will gain the knowledge that you made the challenge and the self-esteem that comes with it. You will learn from the experience, which will help you in subsequent challenges. Finally, it will contribute to the habit of making those challenges, so that in future you won't think about doing it, you will do it automatically.

Emerson says, 'Knowledge is the antidote to fear'. This idea enhances focus. When you focus on doing something correctly, this thought, rather than fear, occupies your mind. If you are afraid of your head clashing with an opponent's when you jump to head the ball, watch what people good at heading the ball do or ask them or a coach to tell you how to protect yourself while trying to win the ball with your head. Whatever part of football you are anxious about, by learning how to perform the skill and focusing on executing it correctly, you increase the unlikelihood that fear will arise because you are acting from a condition of power (knowledge) rather than weakness (ignorance).

As in football, so it is in life. The instinct for self-preservation is at play when you face the challenge of performing in the interview, asking someone out on a date, or submitting your work for judgment in the hope of acceptance and honour. Fear of rejection or getting hurt is what stops many of us from trying to get what we want. We need to focus on performing well or expressing what we are and know, instead of worrying that we might be unsuccessful.

Confidence and courage are closely related. Whereas confidence is more about knowing you can do something, courage is simply focusing on doing what you must do to get what you desire, rather than focusing on the worst-case scenario. For example, most of us would be afraid to run into a burning house and would not bother doing so. But, if a family member or friend were in there, your intense focus on getting them out of the house would override your fear. You would not hesitate.

What this analysis shows is that courage is not a special trait that a few fortunate people are endowed with. Courage is really about what you desire and the strength of your desire. This means that anyone can become courageous. But, it does not mean you will get everything you want in life. No one does. However, a courageous person is likely to get something close to what they want, eventually.

The alternative to a life of courage is a coward's life. A coward must suffer a life of longing, frustration, little value and mediocrity. We want the best things and experiences in life, so cowardice is not an option for us. Therefore, we must strive to become courageous. Courage substantially improves our chances of scoring goals and winning games. More importantly, courage makes possible honour, self-respect and self-reliance.

28

ONLY YOU ARE WITHIN YOUR POWER

IN TENNIS AND golf, you have a high degree of control over each play and the outcome of the contest. In tennis, it is you alone who faces the ball coming over the net and it is up to you to get it back over the net. Roger Federer said this is one of the reasons for him choosing to play tennis instead of football.

In football, we have much less control over the outcome of a match. There are eleven opponents. We also have ten teammates who directly or indirectly affect each play in the game. Even though we want to be in the middle of the action so we can express our skills, often we are frustrated by our opponents, our teammates or what the referee does. The ball might be on the other side of the pitch, so we can't directly influence the game, or a teammate fails to pass us the ball when we are open. These external circumstances can deprive us of the opportunity to directly affect the outcome of the match.

There are two important lessons we can learn from this observation. First, we should not be too attached to the outcome of a football match. It doesn't make sense to pin our hopes on an outcome that we have little control over. For, as the Stoics explain, when we attach our hope to the outcome, we let things outside us dictate whether we are joyful or sad.

We should try to make our emotional experience dependent on what we do and not let external things determine how we feel, for example, the opposition players, our teammates, and the scoring or concession of goals. Hope isn't entirely bad for you, but it is wise to keep your hope in proportion to what you can affect in a game.

This brings us to the second lesson. A fundamental principle of Stoicism is that we should focus only on what is within our power in any given moment of a game. Rather than focus on what our teammate will do, for example, whether they will get the ball to us, focus on what we can do, for example, choose to make the run or go to the ball. If our teammate doesn't get the ball to us, then at least we did the best we could. If our teammate does execute the pass well and we have made the run or gone to the ball, then we are likely to get and keep the ball.

On the other hand, if we focus too much on what our teammate may or may not do, this will affect our decision-making and cause doubt in ourselves and our teammate. We probably won't make a move and so our teammate will have one less option and more pressure. If they do pass the ball well and we don't make the run, then possession will probably be lost, and we will be partly to blame. So, we should focus on what we can do and do it as well as we can. That way we will have no regrets and give ourselves and the team the best chance to make something happen.

Everyday life is more like football than tennis or golf. The outcomes of our long-term plans are at the mercy of many things outside us, for example, the environment and people immediately in our vicinity. One area of life in which this is particularly apparent is parenting. In the earlier years, we can control much of the input that goes into our children's minds. As soon as they start to go to childcare, kindergarten or school, they will spend a lot of time away from us where what happens to them and what influences them will be out of our control.

As in football, the wise approach is to not disproportionately focus on what we hope for our children. Instead, we should focus on what we can do when they are in our presence, where we can directly influence and guide them. This could include controlling what external circumstances we release them into, just as we decide which of our teammates we decide to release the ball to. In a football match, the best we can do is to use all our experience and skill to ensure the ball gets to where we want it to go. Likewise, we can use all our experience and skill to get our children to where we want them to go.

Then again, where the ball ends up will depend on what the recipient does with it. What they do with it depends on the impact on them from other players in the game. It also depends on the environment (for example, the weather and condition of the pitch). The more skilful and experienced the recipient, the more likely the ball will end up in the back of the net. Similarly, we should do the best we can to provide wise guidance and resources to our children so that they are self-reliant and have the power to make good decisions.

This applies to virtually every area of your life. At work you have colleagues, your boss, or your employees and clients, who are external to you and affect the success of your job or business. In love, it is the significant other, their friends and family, perhaps a rival, and your own friends. Your health is influenced by things like the kind of food available, geography and circumstances; for example, whether you must walk or can drive to the supermarket.

The key to scoring goals in all these areas of your life is to focus on what you can do and let go of whatever is beyond your control. You can choose to become skilled, wise and experienced in all these areas of life. By doing so, you will be better equipped to limit your expectations to what is within your power, namely, the ability to choose to express your skill and knowledge as best you can in every moment of the game and then let the external world do as it will. You can hope that members on your team will help you win in the different areas of your life, but remember that much of what happens is beyond your control. Accept this and you will suffer less from fear, regret and disappointment than those who believe they can, and want to, control everything in their lives.

29

PREPARATION TAMES ANXIETY

ANXIETY IS TO some extent constantly present in a player's mind during a game of football. This must be so because a footballer can never know for certain what will happen. Since ignorance begets anxiety, all players feel it to a certain degree. Even the greatest footballers suffer from this destructive feeling. Roberto Baggio in the 1994 World Cup final, Messi in the 2012 Champions League semi-final and Dennis Bergkamp in the 1999 FA Cup semi-final all failed to score from the penalty spot. Fear is often the main cause of an unsuccessful penalty kick.

A part of fear or anxiety is the belief that there is a looming danger. In a game of football, a player must deal with the prospect that their actions are potentially dangerous *or* fruitful. Spinoza would explain that because a footballer cannot know what will happen, doubt invades their mind and anxiety follows it. Hence, a footballer's mind vacillates between hope that their actions will be successful and fear that they will be punished.

For example, goalkeepers fear choosing the wrong way to dive to try to save a goal. Midfielders fear that their pass will be intercepted. Defenders fear that commitment to a tackle might cause a foul to their opponent, or that their opponent will get past them, which might lead to a goal being conceded. And, of course, strikers fear that they will miss the goal. We can see, then, that belief and anxiety are closely connected.

William James, the American psychologist and philosopher, provides the following insight into the nature of belief. Your belief about the outcome makes it happen. If I doubt that I will successfully leap over a chasm, my doubt will be expressed in the emotions of fear and trembling. If I jump in this state, as James says, I'm likely to 'miss my foothold and roll into the abyss'. But, if I believe I will successfully complete the jump, then the fear and trembling will be absent, and my body will function more effectively. That is, according to James, my belief 'creates its own verification'.

In the moment before you take a penalty, there are many thoughts that can pass through your mind. A common unhelpful thought is: what if I miss or the goalkeeper saves it? This thought might come and go quickly, or it might linger. You might contemplate it consciously, but more often it is subconscious. It is expressed in the anxiety you feel or your unrelaxed body. This thought is dangerous, for it augers the likely outcome: that you will miss the penalty shot. Your belief that you will miss makes it true: not the belief itself, but the consequences of the belief, for example, the rigidity and unnatural expression of your body and skill, which express your anxiety.

Players who strongly believe they will score a goal are much more likely to do so. Your beliefs about your abilities are connected to how you feel and act. If you truly believe you will score the penalty, you will be confident and focus on striking the ball with correct technique, rather than on what the goalkeeper is doing or what will happen if you miss. An indecisive player lacks self-belief. A player who lacks self-belief worries about miskicking the ball or their penalty kick being saved. For this reason, the player suffers from anxiety and compromised control over their limbs. Consequently, it is very difficult for a faithless person to focus on performing correct technique. This is the difference between a decisive or calm footballer and a fearful one.

Self-belief or self-confidence (I use these words interchangeably) cannot be switched on or off at will. Self-confidence is difficult to attain, but easily lost. As Arsène Wenger, the former manager of Arsenal, put it, 'You go up by stairs and you come down by the lift'. Even the best players go through phases when they have lost a significant degree of self-confidence. Relative to the amateur, the superstar has greater ability to restore self-belief because they have memories of their numerous past successes to supply them with motivation and fuel their desire to keep trying.

The ability to generate self-belief depends on what you have done to make you what you are today. Messi and Cristiano Ronaldo have played football since they were small and spent many thousands of hours juggling the ball, kicking the ball, and playing football, as well as gaining information from intelligent coaches about what to do in a game. It is no wonder they know that they can complete the pass or put the ball where they want it to go.

The preparation of the great footballers does not only consist of a particular week of training, but all the training and practice they have done and the other games played leading up to the next game. Their preparation is what leads to their self-belief. Because their preparation has been extensive, their self-belief is readily available, whereas the self-belief of an amateur who plays only occasionally will be far weaker and easily crushed by superior players.

Self-confidence is influenced by external factors and circumstances, which are not fully within your power. Being in the final of a World Cup is one of the things that can influence your self-confidence. For example, the pressure of the 1994 World Cup final made Roberto Baggio blast the ball over the goal posts. There is only so much you can do by way of preparation and training that will ensure you will be able to execute your football skills well in a crucial moment of the game. Often an external event, like a penalty kick, can render self-belief extremely vulnerable, no matter how skilful the player. Sometimes self-belief needs assistance.

Understanding the situation and altering your perspective can assist self-belief. Being aware of your perception of others' expectations of you or how much you want to score the goal or to win the game can make you aware of the need to relax and focus only on what you *can* do. Controlling how you feel and what you are thinking in an important moment is very difficult to do. We have some power to place less importance on what other people think of us, particularly if we are self-sufficient or a player who has already achieved a lot. However, toning down your desire in a moment when you could win the World Cup can only be done if you know how you can control your own desires. No one can really explain how to do this.

Taoism provides a solution. According to Taoism, you should not worry about the outcome, whether you score or miss: focus only on expressing (as opposed to performing) your skill and let nature take its course. I say 'express' rather than 'perform' because the latter suggests intention and conscious direction, whereas the former implies that you are manifesting the reality of a part of you. It is the difference between doing something intelligently or skilfully while in a relaxed state rather than in a tense state. The tense approach is us trying too hard, whereas the relaxed approach is us doing what we know how to do with little conscious effort, that is, on autopilot or naturally.

This can be applied to taking a penalty. Rather than being excessively focused on exactly where your foot will strike the ball, exactly how hard, the position of your upper body and the position of the goalkeeper, you will make a spontaneous decision in the moment. You will execute your skill in a relaxed state with conviction rather than blasting it over the goal posts or hitting it tamely. This does not guarantee you will score the goal, but it does ensure that you give your best in the moment. Giving your best will maximise your chances of getting the ball past the goalkeeper, but it also has at least two other benefits.

One is that it will force the goalkeeper to pull off a terrific save. Instead of your howler living in the spectators' memories, it will be an amazing save. This isn't ideal, but it's nice and the sign of a wise and self-sufficient person to recognise the ability or achievements of others. The other benefit is that you will not live with regret or repeatedly berate yourself for your error. So, acting without effort or spontaneously and not thinking of the outcome is the key to expressing your power to the highest degree.

Consider what it means if you do not do this and do the opposite. It means you think you are a god or that you can control everything in the world. This is delusional thinking. You cannot have absolute control of the ball. You cannot control the goalkeeper. You cannot even control exactly what you are going to do all the time. So, if you take this approach, you allow your desperation to win to determine what you do and, thus, the consequences of what you do.

There is a whole world outside you made up of an infinite number of things. Any one of these could interfere with what you do, and hence, whether you achieve your aim: from an uneven patch of turf to a spontaneous thought in your own mind. Having perspective about where you fit in the scheme of things and controlling your ego can not only help you forestall unnecessary egotistical self-criticism, but improve your chances of achieving positive results; for example, slotting the ball in the corner of the net.

Preparation is essential to success in all human activities. It could be a job interview, a school interview, a presentation, a try out for a part in a movie or a band, or even a date. To succeed in these activities, you must be able to perform the skills of the role to the standard required by your judges. As in football, the best approach is the way of the Tao. Put simply, you should go with the flow, stick to what you know and forget about the judges and the outcome. You will relax and, as a result, act more naturally.

You should be honest with yourself about your abilities. If you have good reasons for thinking you can fulfil the role, then trust in your preparation, and instead of anxiety predominating in your mind, you will focus on doing the task at hand to the best of your present ability. You might not get the result you want. The best response to a bad outcome is to subsequently strive to increase your ability and practice putting yourself in a relaxed state. A relaxed state maximises the expression of your abilities.

In football and other areas of life, anxiety indicates unpreparedness, self-doubt and fear of not getting what you want. In a game you are participating in, you can deal with anxiety in the following way. Try to relax and focus on performing your skills correctly. Accept that relaxation and focus might not be enough to get you the result you want in the present game. Then you can treat the present game as a practice session, even if it is a proper or serious game. Try to play well in a relaxed state but resolve to do better in the next game.

In general, the best strategy is to not worry about what will happen or try too hard to control yourself or the game. Your preparation will ensure that you act correctly.

30

PEOPLE TEND TO FORGET THEIR ORIGINS

TALENT CAN APPEAR inborn. One player struggles to perform a basic skill like passing the ball and another seems to execute the fundamentals effortlessly. Many footballers are reluctant to give less competent players a chance by not passing them the ball or refusing to let them on their team. Typically, we don't give a person time to show us their abilities. We tend to judge another footballer's level of skill and ability instantly.

In general, people don't think about the other person's experiences and opportunities, or lack thereof, that have moulded them into the person they are in the present moment. Most people forget the time and effort they have put into developing their *own* skills and abilities. Players like Messi, Neymar, Pele and Maradona played football every day. Even players on your own team who have great ability practiced their skills continually and played football regularly.

When we judge a player as they presently appear to us, we undervalue their potential. Sure, if you are assessing players for an immediate game, it is best to judge a person's ability by what they can do now. But, when we first meet a player we should not judge them absolutely, for often our judgment stubbornly clings to the mind afterwards. As a result, not only do we mistreat the player, we might incorrectly judge that this is all the person can or might ever do. It can blind us to the positive attributes and skills they do have or their potential to become a good footballer, which might not have shone the first time we met them. They might be able to become a good footballer, but because of our impatience, we are oblivious to the evidence of their potential.

People usually do not think about how people come to be what they are. Rather, they judge them as they are now. That is fine. Most people are impatient, and thinking is hard. Considering why this person has exactly the level of skill they do is too much work. However, if you are someone who prides themselves on being fair to others or attracting the best, then try to break the habit of making absolute judgments based on your first impression.

Just as we often instantly judge the ability of new footballers, so we do in most areas of life. This attitude is prevalent in the field of education. People are often judged stupid, uneducated or poorly educated if they don't know some fact or theory, haven't heard of some idea, don't understand the meaning of some word like *aretai* (I remember philosophy students sniggering because I didn't know what this meant) or have difficulty articulating their thoughts.

A judgmental person usually forms the false assumption that because another person doesn't know x, that makes the knowing person smarter than the other. What the judgemental person fails to recognise is that their knowledge of the fact, theory or meaning associated with a word was not always part of the body of knowledge that constitutes their present intellect. They had to look in a dictionary or have someone explain the meaning of the word. If the person judged harshly looked in the dictionary or had someone correctly explain the word, then they would understand the word as well.

I put this idea to one of my tutors in law school. In response, he said if someone asks him for advice about some legal issue, he doesn't have to look in a book to find the answer. He just knows the answer, which makes him more knowledgeable than that person. This is true from a certain perspective, but his answer also reveals that he is somewhat naïve.

His answer suggests he believed he was gifted with legal knowledge and that this gift makes him superior to others. In fact, this tutor liked to belittle people in class who didn't know the answers to questions that he judged to be obvious. It did not occur to him that the legal knowledge he possessed resulted from study and learning from law textbooks and lecturers. It is interesting that a tutor in law in a university can have such a conceited and limited view of the origin of his legal knowledge and his level of intelligence relative to other people.

What people say or do in each moment reflects only a fraction of their current ability and potential. Rather than dismiss, mock or criticise a person's actions that do not measure up to your standard, have the idea ready at hand that this person's current level of skill is not fixed, nor have they always been this way. This can help us to feel less intimidated by people we meet who have exceptional talent, but it can also make us more understanding and supportive of those whose abilities do not stand out.

Yet, there is nothing wrong with having high standards. At a club like Real Madrid, what a player can do now is all that matters. This suggests that we should factor the nature of the situation into our assessment of a person's credentials. If it's a big club or an important job, then we are right to tell the person without the requisite level of ability that they are unqualified and so, presently, they must be rejected.

This should not stop us from supporting unready or unqualified candidates by providing realistic feedback. The person's expectations might be extremely unrealistic. Rather than ridiculing the person's attempt to make the team, we can provide them with personalised and reasonable advice. This can make the difference between the person losing all hope or striving to improve and persisting. By reminding yourself of your own humble origins, the mistakes you made and corrections of your efforts by others, you can see the person in front of you not only as a hopeful applicant, but also as a fellow human being with potential.

This perspective can engender within us humility, self-awareness and empathy. If we want to be good people and help make the world a better place, then we must avoid measuring others by our own current skill level and acknowledge that the other person has the potential to learn and develop their skills.

31

THE GAME WILL NOT STOP FOR YOU

ONCE THE REFEREE blows the whistle, the game is on. If you are one of the players on the pitch, then unless you are injured, get a red card or walk off, you are stuck in the game. What I'm interested in here is the state of mind a player might have when the game isn't unfolding the way they would like it to.

Perhaps they are not playing well, teammates are underperforming, or the referee is making terrible decisions. Players in this kind of situation might feel like giving up and unleashing frustration on teammates, the opposition, the referee, the fans or themselves. A player might feel powerless to do anything and give up hope of playing the game well or that things will ever go their way.

In this situation, imagine you did nothing and just stood still. What would happen? The game would carry on, whatever you did. This would annoy your teammates, and rightly so. It is a team sport and you are part of the team, so you are expected to contribute to the efforts of your team. Further, the opposition will exploit this weakness. And, if you continue to despair that things aren't going your way, then your unpleasant state will rob you of any fun and satisfaction you might get from simply accepting the circumstances and going with the flow.

Let us consider what would happen if you went with the flow. The first consequence is that you would now be in a more positive state. You wouldn't be resistant or tense. In your previous state, you would have been more vulnerable to making an error when you tried to control or pass the ball. By going with the flow, you would be less worried about the mistakes you, your teammates or the referee might be making and more focused on what you could do. In this frame of mind, you would let the game come to you instead of trying to control the overall game, which is beyond your power.

You should accept that a game has a certain momentum of its own. For example, the opposition is totally dominating your team. In these circumstances, rather than focusing on what you cannot control, like the momentum of the game, your teammates and the referee, you free yourself to play your own game. This has a knock-on effect. Your positive state will increase the likelihood that your next play will be more effective. You are more likely to retain possession. You will tend to pass the ball more confidently and your successful passes will tend to put your teammates in a better position to make a good play. So, by going with the flow you give a positive impetus to your team.

Real life has its own momentum. Government policies and actions, economic forces, employers, family and friends affect us in numerous ways. A regulation may change forcing you to pay for parking at your place of employment. Employers may be struggling, so they can't offer you work. Unfortunate circumstances like these can infuriate us or make us want to stop playing the game of life. However, it is better to go with the flow and do the best you can with what you have, rather than worrying about the people and forces outside you that you cannot control.

Consider the example of a loved one who isn't doing what you think is best for them or their family. A family member might have a serious problem like drug addiction. Getting angry or upset isn't by itself going to stop your loved one from taking drugs or stop them doing something you think is harmful. Your anger only really affects you, and in a bad way. Your anger and frustration will make it difficult for you to see things more clearly. This lack of clarity is likely to taint the effectiveness of your actions.

You might try to pressure your loved one to stop taking drugs, but this confrontation is likely to go against the loved one's momentum, that is, you are likely to be perceived as a barrier to the satisfaction of their desire. If so, they will treat you as an obstacle that needs to be avoided or broken down. This doesn't mean you should give up on people in need of help or allow others you care about to harm themselves. In football, one player is unlikely to beat the whole team of the opposition. Likewise, you may need support that is presently unavailable to help the person you care about.

It may be more prudent to go with the flow until circumstances change in a way that make it easier for you to help your family member, friend or someone you care about. By taking this approach, you are not fighting against the tide and you restore your power. Accept that other people won't always do what you want them to do. They need to be ready and willing to change themselves. Life will continue relentlessly whatever you do. So, you should go with the flow and wait for an opportune moment to attempt to influence the game in a positive way.

32

SUFFERING IS A NATURAL PART OF THE GAME

DISAPPOINTMENT, FRUSTRATION, ANGER and suffering are natural consequences of playing football. These emotions are inescapable because we want something outside ourselves that is beyond our absolute control, namely, success and victory.

Spinoza's insight into the nature of human emotions explains why this is so. Our desires express our nature, which is the power by which we strive to preserve ourselves. Our nature is common to all things in the universe. All things, be they human beings, animals, plants and everything else, are composed of this power, which can be understood as a thing's inherent *tendency* for self-preservation. I say 'tendency' here because the word 'instinct' seems inapplicable to things like water, rocks, and stars.

The power that constitutes our very nature is part of the whole universe. In other words, you are part of the *power* of the universe. According to Spinoza, our natural power *is* our very life and our emotions express the agitations of our life force. Our emotions, explains Spinoza, provide us with feedback about how our body is affected by things outside us. Human emotion is like a fuel gauge in that it informs us of the level of our natural power.

This suggests that the emotions reflect the unity of an individual human's mind and body. The neuroscientist Antonio Damasio praises Spinoza because he was one of the few philosophers (prior to 20th century science) to understand that the human mind is not something independent of the body. The foundation of human emotions or feelings *is* the body. Our emotional experiences reflect the way in which the life *or* power of our body is affected by things external to us.

Desire, joy and sadness, says Spinoza, are the basic emotions that express natural human power. When we feel sad, our desire, which is the emotional expression of the power by which we strive to preserve ourselves and increase our power, is weakened in that our striving or desire has been obstructed or frustrated. When we feel joy, our power or desire is strengthened, for our power or desire to preserve ourselves has been aided or satisfied.

What this means is that our natural or personal power is diminished when our desires are frustrated, and this is experienced as the feeling of sadness. The satisfaction of our desires increases our natural or personal power, and this is experienced as the feeling of joy. So, when we score a goal, win a football match or get anything we want in life, we experience joy because our desire for these things has been satisfied or our personal power has increased. In other words, joy is power. But, when we lose a football match, are rejected, or do not get what we want, we experience sadness because our desire for these things was frustrated or our personal power was diminished. Therefore, sadness means you are in a weakened state.

In football, many events will occur that are contrary to our desires: misplaced passes, miscommunication, bad decisions by the referee, not getting the ball when you are open, miskicks, poor goalkeeping, and, ultimately, losing the game. To desire these things is to invite suffering because our power to attain them is limited and whether we do obtain them depends on many things outside our control.

Every day is a source of disappointment and frustration. Even on our best days some things occur that are opposed to our desires. Sometimes we get what we strongly desire. In accord with Spinoza's theory of the emotions, this causes in us an elevated level of joy, which can overpower minor frustrations of our desires. Scoring the winning goal in a football match, kissing a girl or guy you are crazy about or getting the job you always wanted can fill you with so much joy that your light-headedness will make you overlook the bad pass, your date's narcissism or perhaps the rudeness of a member on the interview panel.

When things happen that are contrary to our strongest desires, every annoyance or minor frustration of desire is exacerbated. In the case of a bad pass that leads to the waste of an opportunity to win the match, your sadness, frustration and anger associated with that teammate will be compounded. If your date informs you that they are not really interested in you, their vanity will now annoy you. If you don't get the job, then your disappointment will magnify the rudeness of the interviewer and intensify your feeling of indignation. When we are sad, that is, we don't get what we want, it is hard not to have a bleak view of everything in life.

Accept that suffering is the price to be paid for wanting anything in life. We cannot realistically expect to always feel joyful because the world has not been set up solely to satisfy our desires. Every other person has their own desires and views about how the world should be. It is ignorant and narrow-minded to believe we should not be unhappy. The world does not owe us anything and most of the time everyone is thinking mainly about themselves.

The solution to the existence of suffering is to accept and acknowledge it. By understanding the cause of the most common kind of human suffering, namely, the frustration of our desires, we can consciously try to moderate our desires and expectations. Recognition that profound suffering must follow frustration of strong desire can enable us to respond intelligently to our suffering. For example, rather than dwelling on a loss, we accept it and focus on the next match. This makes it easy to understand why philosophies like Buddhism, Spinozism and Stoicism teach the principle of non-attachment to things beyond our power.

In addition to moderating our desires, a useful strategy for dealing with suffering in life is to apply the advice of Arthur Schopenhauer, the 19th century German philosopher. Rather than seeing other people as companions of happiness, we should view them as *fellow sufferers*, or *companions of misery*. I would add that we should take this approach while being hopeful, encouraging and acknowledging the good in the world.

Schopenhauer's advice is helpful for the following reason. What most of us can relate to is suffering because every day some of our desires are frustrated. In a football match, we can commiserate with teammates or opponents who suffer because of a mistake they made or even an unfortunate injury. Rather than always speaking of our successes or expecting others to, let us acknowledge and fully witness the suffering of our fellow human beings in our day-to-day lives, not in the sense of *schadenfreude* or in a sanctimonious way, but in a thoughtful and empathetic manner.

Suffering is a common experience, but try not to see it as a competition. Some of us try to make ourselves feel special by recounting how terrible our lives have been. Suffering is not something to be praised. We should acknowledge and accept suffering when we cannot avoid it. Suffering is simply to be brought into view, rather than pretending it does not exist or avoiding talking about it because it is unpleasant. This can help us feel more connected to each other.

33

THE JOURNEY MAKES THE GREATEST JOY POSSIBLE

I HATE BEING told the result of a football match I intend to watch later. Unlike me, some people just want to know if their team won or not. They think that you shouldn't be upset by learning the final score. What these people fail to realise is that knowing the final score is less valuable than watching the game from beginning to end. Watching the whole game without knowing the outcome makes it possible for the drama of the game to affect you profoundly.

What matters when watching a football match is the emotional journey. A live football match has greater power to maximise the joy of watching your team score the winner, the fury at a penalty or free kick wrongly awarded against your team, or the exhilaration of seeing your favourite player unexpectedly do something amazing, like sending the ball into the back of the net from a free kick. If you know the result and who scored, then the strength of the emotions that you can experience will be greatly diminished. Experiencing the rollercoaster of emotions is what makes watching the match worthwhile.

Suppose you were told the result of every game you played in life: the game of love, the game of work, the game of parenting and the game of friendship. Let's focus on the game of love for a moment. Imagine you knew whether a girl or guy would say yes or no to you. You might think that would be preferable, for that would remove your anxiety. There are two points to make about this way of thinking.

First, anxiety is an important feeling. It makes you aware of the gravity of the situation. Anxiety indicates that much is at stake: your own sense of self-worth and happiness, to begin with. If you eliminated anxiety, you would also take away the meaning associated with having the partner you want. That is, it would undermine the importance to you of the person choosing you.

Second, if you knew what this person would say, you wouldn't experience the intense joy that would follow if they accepted your advances. Of course, you also wouldn't experience the overwhelming sadness if they rejected you. But, the sadness and the joy go hand in hand. You can't have one without the potential for the other.

This raises an interesting issue. Long-term relationships, particularly marriage, are a constant reminder of the result of the game of love. You know what your partner said, and maybe you wish the result were different, but you live with the result every day you stay with the person. This means your chances of experiencing the heights of joy (and depths of sadness) connected with early love are not going to be reignited.

No wonder many people live in loveless and unhappy marriages. It would be like watching a rerun of a game of football in which your team won again, and again, and again. Marriages are not like reruns, for you might find new issues to argue about. Since it's the journey that matters and knowing the result negatively impacts the journey, you should ask yourself if you want to know the result. In the case of your long-term relationship, do you want to be with the same person for the rest of your life? Maybe you do and maybe you don't. That is for you to decide.

The wise thing to do, then, is to embrace the unknown. This is contrary to the security we feel when we know what will happen. We want security, but with security comes a loss of emotional experience. Remind yourself that for you to experience the greatest possible feeling of joy caused by the person you like choosing you, you need to accept that you can't know (and shouldn't want to know if you could) the outcome. Go with the flow and embrace the journey.

We imagine that it would be best to know how to predict and control the outcome. This knowledge would deprive us of much of the meaning, emotional experience and lessons we could learn from doing our best without knowing what will happen. Don't worry about what will happen tomorrow. Focus on now, this moment, which is a single step on your life journey.

34

IT IS UP TO YOU TO DECIDE TO APPRECIATE A MOMENT

PERHAPS THE GREATEST ambition of a footballer is to play in a final, or even a game that will decide the title. Not everyone gets the opportunity to reach this level and, if you do, it might be your only one. There are great players who never played in a final who were worthy of having done so, but because of missed opportunities in a game or not being on a strong enough team, they missed out.

At every level of football, there are excellent players who were denied the opportunity to play on the biggest stage. The Portuguese footballer Eusébio and the Welshman Ryan Giggs are two of the best players in the world who never appeared in a World Cup final. Giggs never even qualified for the tournament with his country. There have been players on amateur teams who were very talented, but their team was not good enough to make it to the final of their competition. So, if you reach the final of a competition you should wholly immerse yourself in it and be grateful that you have been given the opportunity. Focus on this game for the whole ninety minutes and give everything you have so you will have no regrets.

Many moments in our ordinary lives are great opportunities that may never come again. Some people may never have the opportunity that has been presented to you. It could be an interview for an amazing job, the opportunity to see a musician or a play, a one show only event, the first date with someone who you really connect with, or it could be the moments that make up your child's childhood. Many people strongly desire to experience these precious moments and are worthy of them, but they will not have the opportunity to do so.

The likelihood of success in football parallels the likelihood of success in the current employment market. Many people are equally skilled, but because there are only a few positions, almost all must be rejected. Success in romantic relationships is likewise subject to the whim of fortune. A couple deeply in love might be torn apart by circumstances; for example, a visa has expired, or one of them must move interstate or overseas for some reason. Some people can't have children because they are infertile. So, if you get the interview or job, the satisfying relationship, or become pregnant, understand that you are getting to do or have something that not everyone gets to do or have, and you might not get the opportunity again.

Make the most of the special moment. Remind yourself that this moment is happening and that it might never happen again. Focus on doing well. Act with all the energy and positivity you can muster. In an interview, instead of wondering about whether you will be accepted or rejected, decide to enjoy the moment, perform your skills as well as you can and say the things that you believe will present you as the best person for the job. If you are with someone you like and you want to express how you feel about them, make yourself tell them. If your son or daughter wants you to play with them or spend time with them, do it, make the most of it and be fully present. The moment will come and go like a blossom carried away by the wind.

God is not going to freeze time, throw the spotlight on you and your special moment, descend from heaven to the music of angels, shake your hand and declare that this is a special moment and that it ought to be celebrated and remembered for eternity. You must decide to do this yourself. It is easy to take things for granted and waste or fail to appreciate special moments. To make the most of your life and wring as much joy and meaning as you can out of it, get into the habit of recognising when a special moment has arrived in your life and then totally immerse yourself in it. Appreciate the moment—you might never get another like it again.

35

SELF-MASTERY IS THE HIGHEST GOOD

IN FOOTBALL AND life, self-mastery is the source of real power. It enables you to perform your skills correctly, at will. Not only does a master have the power to control their game, the exercise and awareness of self-mastery creates a feeling of joy. Thus, self-mastery is the cause of self-esteem.

The attainment of self-mastery in football is a simple process, but extremely difficult to achieve, for to achieve it, all you need to do is to learn the correct techniques, routinely practice them often and constantly play football. A footballer has achieved self-mastery when they always know what to do, when and how to do it, and do it.

Self-mastery is difficult to achieve for many reasons. Not everyone has access to the best coaches, strong enough motivation, or opportunities to practice and play football regularly. Some players miss out on the opportunity to become masters because they live in remote or disadvantaged areas, but they have as much potential as the player scouted by big clubs in Europe or well-known football academies.

This is true of everyday life. Virtually every human being has the potential to master their own lives and to realise the life they imagine for themselves, but not everyone is lucky enough to have the best teachers, great opportunities and people willing to help them improve themselves.

There are many things outside our power, what we call luck or fortune, that determine whether a person becomes a master in football or life. Still, if we want to experience the best of what football or life offers us, we need to gain knowledge of human nature, and develop our football or life skills. Then we must consistently practice the skills and use our insight into human nature to guide our decision-making if we are to become masters of football or our own lives. Self-mastery is worthwhile because it makes it possible for us to play the game beautifully.

There have been many masters of the game of football. Pele, Maradona, Messi and, my favourite, the Brazilian Ronaldo, are four of the greatest to play the game. It is easy to see that these divine footballers are different from the rest of the highly skilled players on the pitch. The masters show us what is achievable in football. They command respect from their opponents, their teammates and their fans. Their ability to do what they want with the ball and to be able to dominate a game puts fear in the opposition, hope and confidence in their teammates and a sense of anticipation in their fans. These are nice consequences of mastery, but mastery is to be highly valued because of the personal power it generates in the player. A master seems to have a godlike power to influence the game.

It is undeniable that there are games when the masters look ordinary. They underperform or fail to do what is expected of them. Even Ronaldo went more than a few games without scoring a goal (and, no, it wasn't due to injury). In some games, their mastery appears to have deserted them, but their skills and knowledge are unchanged. Unlike isolated masters, like artists and writers, a footballer must execute their skills while under great pressure, which depends on the health and fitness of the body, how tired they are, the intensity of their opponents and the importance of the moment. So, *execution* of mastery has a lot to do with luck or things outside a player's control. Self-mastery does not mean you always do or get what you want, but it does mean you have the ability to do or get what you want.

Mastery of your own life is much like mastery of football in that the performance of skills must usually be done under pressure. In an interview, you must deal with how you are feeling at the time, the mood or tone of those interviewing you and any unexpected questions they ask. When disciplining a child, you must deal with the emotions that arise in you, the child and any other person involved at the time, as well as the child's level of understanding, and the context, for example, in public or at home. Being a master player does not eliminate pressure or guarantee you will get what you want, but it increases the likelihood that you will do what you want to do or get what you want.

How do you become a master in football or life? The answer is hard work. You must acquire knowledge of the game, learn the skills and then practice them tirelessly. If you want to be a true master, you must devote more time than most people are prepared to, but you also must admit to yourself that you are flawed and have much to learn. No matter how much you have learned and improved, like the masters of football, you will continue to make mistakes, which you can learn from.

True masters are never content with their understanding and skill level. They are always striving to improve themselves. By contrast, many of us do not deliberately strive to master our own lives. And most of us are disinclined to admit our imperfections to ourselves, let alone anyone else. This explains why there are so few masters of their own lives.

For those of us who want to master our lives so we can play the game of life beautifully, we need many aids to achieve self-mastery. In football, we need good coaches to teach us the skills and strategies needed to win a game. A good coach sets up drills for us to develop our skills and monitors our performance to identify our strengths and weaknesses. We need life coaches or mentors to do the same for us in the other areas of our lives.

Life coaches can come in the form of actual people, books or other media. In everyday life, there are people we might know who are good at their jobs, good at managing family relations, have good friendships, are financially well off or are good communicators. If you are fortunate enough to personally know such people, spend time with them and try to learn from them. Ask them for advice and then apply it. You could even ask them to suggest some drills, that is, practices and routines to help you improve your skills in a certain area of your life. Alternatively, seek wisdom and advice in self-help or personal development books, autobiographies, interviews with successful people and so on.

No matter what you want in life, you need the *ability* to do the things that will get you what you want. You need personal power and this arises from self-mastery. It takes a long time, discipline, perseverance and help from wise people to achieve self-mastery. Yet, every human being has the potential to master their own lives, since all human beings can learn and improve themselves. You can play the game of life beautifully because within you exists the power to master your own life.

PART FIVE
THE BEAUTIFUL GAME

BARCELONA AND THE national team of Brazil have dazzled fans with breathtaking football. Individual performances like the Brazilian Ronaldo's against Manchester United in the 2002–03 Champions League quarter-final and Zidane's against Brazil in the 1998 World Cup final glued our eyes to the pitch or television screens. There are the great goals of the World Cup. In 1986, Maradona cut through the whole English national team and in 2014 James Rodríguez scored a goal that required him to control the ball with his chest, pivot and volley the ball from outside the 18-yard box. There are the outstanding saves by goalkeepers, game winning tackles, and wild flicks that cut open a defence. These moments of genius inspire in us love for the game of football and make it appear as something more than mere mortals kicking a ball around on a patch of grass.

Beauty exists in all areas of life. Playing the game of life well can inspire the same kind of reactions as beautiful football. Making a real connection to other people, acts of kindness, risking our lives for the wellbeing of others, standing up for what we believe is right, as well as the splendour of the natural world, are instances of beauty that exist in life that any human being can behold and appreciate.

We should try to play football and the game of life beautifully. When we don't have the opportunity to do so ourselves, we can at least acknowledge beauty when we see it and give thanks to those who have exhibited it. We can appreciate beauty for its own sake and so make our own life experiences more enjoyable. Just as we love to see football played beautifully as much (or nearly as much) as we want our team to win or favourite player to excel, beautiful performances in the game of life can take our mind off our narrow self-interests (at least for a while), enabling us to enjoy the journey, rather than always standing on tiptoe to see what life has in store for us.

36

BEAUTY EXPRESSES EXCELLENCE

THE BEST FOOTBALL is beautiful football. An individual dribbling the ball past several players, launching a pin-point accurate 40-yard pass, or curling the ball around the goalkeeper from outside the 18-yard box can all inspire admiration in the fans. Perhaps the game is most beautiful when the whole team is involved in the construction of a sequence of passes that leads to a goal, like the one scored by the Argentinian national team against Serbia and Montenegro in the 2006 World Cup. Cambiasso finished off a breathtaking sequence of twenty-five passes.

Like football, life can show its beauty through the actions of a single human being or through the collective efforts of many. Nelson Mandela, former president of South Africa, forgave his oppressors, which inspired many people around the world to become more tolerant and forgiving of others. The world's compassionate response to the aftermath of the tsunami in South-East Asia in 2004 showed us humanity at its best and most beautiful.

The world is full of interesting and amazing people who create beauty in the world. Beauty can be seen in the everyday acts of kindness that do not make the news but leave an indelible mark on the recipient of the kindness. When life seems ugly and not worth living, rather than lamenting the absence of people playing the game of life beautifully, you can do so yourself. You can be kind, even though you feel miserable. Lending a hand, listening attentively and sincerely, or substituting judgment for an attempt to understand another person, are actions that express the better part of human nature. Rather than despairing of our fellow humans living up to the best of which they are capable, we can instead be generous and kind to them.

René Descartes, the 17th century French philosopher, said that generous people are those who know that the only thing truly in their power is their choices. Generous people strive to make the best choices they can. Conversely, ungenerous people make bad choices, which usually causes trouble for themselves and other people. Descartes believed that generous people understand that the wrongdoing of other people occurs because they are guided by bad ideas.

The greatest philosophers teach that excellence of character is expressed through actions that are both wise and kind. So, instead of judging others harshly, we should act generously by doing what we judge is best. Sometimes many people cooperate to make life seem wonderful, but every act of generosity adds to the experience of beauty in life, even though it is witnessed by few or only a single soul. It can be up to you to decide if in this moment beauty is present and outshines any negativity.

37

CREATIVITY IS UNORIGINAL

CREATIVE ABILITY TURNS mortals into gods worshipped by fans of the beautiful game. The ability to create something unexpected is the reason clubs like Paris St Germain will pay over $300 million for a player as talented as Neymar.

The genius of master footballers is not inborn. Their genius is the result of study, imitation and repetition of skill. Every footballing genius laboriously studied the masters who preceded them. As Emerson says: 'If we require the originality which consists in weaving, like a spider, their web from their own bowels; in finding clay, and making bricks, and building the house; no great men are original'. Even the first footballer had to get inspiration to do a stepover from somewhere, be it an accident or some other experience.

This is true in all areas of human creativity, for as the greatest philosophers have taught, nothing can come from nothing. For example, according to Ip Man, the famous Wing Chun master and teacher of Bruce Lee, Ng Mui, a Buddhist nun, originated the Wing Chun system of martial art. Ng Mui's creation of this new style of martial art arose from her observing a snake and a crane fighting. So, Ng Mui did not derive this new style entirely from herself, but she developed it into a powerful martial art.

Wing Chun was the foundation of Bruce Lee's fighting skill. Bruce Lee himself was indebted, not only to his teacher Ip Man, but also to the masters of other styles from whom he learned, and his study of martial arts and philosophy. Even though Bruce Lee's debt to his forebears and certain contemporary martial artists was considerable, his creative power was so great that he inspired, and continues to inspire, millions of people around the world to learn martial arts and follow his example.

The indebtedness of genius does not degrade its value, for it still has the power to create and the power to produce joy in us. This insight should be welcomed because it shows that almost anyone can develop the ability to be creative in football or other areas of life. It is possible because in football, for example, the flicks, the stepover and the volley are skills that can be learned.

Several factors give rise to creativity. There are practical and emotional factors. Practical factors include mastery of the basic skills, knowledge of the game and ability to imagine in advance what you can do. Emotional factors comprise desire, love and self-confidence.

The emotional side of creativity is most important. You need to love football and desire to play the game as often as possible. If you desire to play and love to play, then you will always be seeking opportunities to play. The more you play, the more you will understand the game, learn to read the game and develop your skills. A side effect of our love or desire for something is that we tend to remember those things more clearly that are connected to strong emotion. So, if you really love football, the knowledge of the game and the skills you learn are more likely to stick. Your self-confidence will grow and this will increase your willingness to try to create an unanticipated opportunity to beat a player or score a goal.

A player that desires and loves to play football will continually develop their skills and ability to read the game. Once you have a good understanding of the game and have some ability to perform the skills at will, you will have self-belief, that is, you will believe that you can do what you want to do and perform the skills when you want to. Naturally, you will continually try to be creative during a game of football.

None of the superstars pull off the tricks every time though. They often make mistakes. On their way to developing the ability to perform the tricks, they messed them up many times. A moment of genius in football could easily have resulted in embarrassment and frustration for the player, their teammates and the fans.

Creativity is valuable in many areas of life. The act of writing often involves considerable scope for creativity. An examiner of my Master's thesis commented that I have 'a real knack for creative reading'. He was referring to my interpretation of Spinoza's philosophy and the arguments I made based on it. What enabled me to do this was my love of Spinoza and his philosophy. My love motivated me to read all of Spinoza's works and to think carefully about how the various parts of his philosophy fit together. This enabled me to draw on the various parts to present possible solutions to interpretive puzzles.

This principle is applicable to all kinds of activity, be it conversation, writing fiction or non-fiction, art, debate, any of the professions and even dating. If you love the game of life or any part of it, as much as someone like Messi loves football, then you will seek out good teachers who will impart the fundamentals to you and teach you the tricks of the game. You will train and play whenever you can and, consequently, you will deeply understand the game and your skills will be finely tuned. Creative ability enables you to exploit, in an unexpected way, even the slightest opportunity that arises in a game you are playing.

38

WITHOUT THE ORDINARY, THERE CAN BE NO EXTRAORDINARY

ONE OF THE best football matches was the 1999 Champions League final between Manchester United and Bayern Munich. In the last few minutes of the game, I was confident Bayern would win, even though United were relentless. When the first United goal went in to make it 1-1, I thought the game would go into extra time, but destiny was on United's side. Two goals in the space of a few minutes, in injury time, wrested the victory from Bayern.

United achieved one of the greatest comebacks in football. Other equally astonishing feats include Liverpool's comeback against Milan in the 2005 Champions League final from 3-0 down and Manchester City winning the Premier League title in 2011–12 in the fourth minute of injury time in the last game of the season. These amazing football games and surprise endings inspire us and excite our imaginations.

Not all football matches are dramatic and compelling. Most matches are ordinary, and many are tedious. There are more 0-0 draws than we would like and games in which there are few actual shots on goal. This should not make us lose interest in football, however. At any moment a football match might produce something special, an act of genius, like

Clarence Seedorf's astounding 45-yard strike for Real Madrid against Atlético Madrid in 1997.

Imagine if, just before Seedorf used his football magic, you decided that the game was not living up to your expectations and stopped watching or, you were a Manchester United supporter and in the ninetieth minute switched off the television. I'm sure that some fans did exactly that. People who did this missed out on witnessing the creation of a football legend.

The problem is that we are often too impatient or lack faith and so we lose interest quickly or give up on ourselves or our team. To experience the best of what football offers, you must take the ordinary and mediocre as well. Of course, you could save time and frustration by watching the highlights, but the experience and the feelings of astonishment, wonder, disbelief and ecstasy will not be available for you to enjoy, or, if you do, your experience of them will be greatly diminished.

Life is full of special moments and surprise outcomes. The partner of your dreams might be just around the corner. A friend of mine used to say that there will be a day before the day that you will meet the girl you have been searching for. What if on the day before you meet that girl or guy, you simply give up? The day before a party you are invited to, you despair of ever finding a partner you can connect with, and being depressed, you decide to not attend the party. But, there was a girl or guy there who you would have connected with. It would be like the Manchester United players giving up in the ninetieth minute. Unbeknown to them, their seemingly impossible dream, in that moment, was achievable, but if they had given up before the final whistle was blown, not only would they have missed out on earning the victory, they would never have known how close they were to accomplishing something extraordinary.

This applies to making new friends, creating that business you have envisioned or embarking on and succeeding in that career you feel you were made for. The monotony of everyday life and our repeated efforts and actions that do not bear fruit are like 0-0 football matches. In these moments we should remind ourselves why we love the game of life so much. The beauty, magic and moments of genius that are possible in life should motivate us to remain engaged. While you continue playing the game, there is the possibility that life will surprise you.

39

RESOLUTION CONQUERS ADVERSITY

ONE OF THE most beautiful things in life is the triumph of the human spirit. The Brazilian Ronaldo achieved one of the greatest spiritual triumphs in football. After a series of horrific injuries, many observers thought he was finished. Most commentators judged that the best player in the world, and in my view, potentially the greatest of all time, would never climb to the heights he attained before his injuries. Just before the 2002 World Cup, little was expected from a player once universally known as 'The Phenomenon', the most exciting footballer in the world.

Injuries bedevilled Ronaldo throughout his career. Perhaps the most serious and career-defining were the knee injuries he suffered while playing for Inter Milan. Early in the 1999–2000 season, he injured his right knee, and required surgery. Consequently, he was out of action for almost five months of the season. He worked hard to return to the game he loved and dominated. Having followed his doctors' orders and done everything in his power to get himself match-ready, he returned to play for Inter against Lazio in the first leg of the 2000 Coppa Italia final.

Less than eight minutes after his substitution into the game, his right knee collapsed while he was attacking with the ball at his feet. Ronaldo was in agony. The agony would also be felt in terms of the ruination of all his hard work to rehabilitate his knee and the likelihood that his career as a footballer was finished.

Unusually, Brazil was not a top favourite to win the 2002 World Cup. At one point in the qualification stage, it appeared that the then four-times world champions were at risk of losing their record of being the only national team to have participated in every World Cup tournament. Prior to the World Cup, Ronaldo had little preparation. He had missed the best part of three seasons of football and the qualification campaign. Everyone knew what he had achieved prior to his setbacks, but with so little game time and his crippling injuries, few thought he would be able to return to his best. Most commentators perceived Ronaldo's attempt at a comeback sympathetically, but they expected more disappointment for him. They did not know that he was destined to show the world that he was still 'The Phenomenon'.

Ronaldo helped Brazil win all seven matches and their fifth World Cup. He scored in every game except the one against England on the way to the final. He scored two goals in the final and could easily have scored four or five. Ronaldo was the player of the final and the leading scorer of the World Cup, with eight goals in seven games, the highest number of goals scored by an individual player in a World Cup for decades. 'The Phenomenon' reminded the world that he was a special player and proved his doubters wrong.

Following his World Cup triumph, Ronaldo won the FIFA World Player of the Year award. He was transferred to Real Madrid and was a member of the original Galácticos, one of the most talented football teams ever assembled, with Zidane, Raúl, Figo, Beckham (eventually) and Roberto Carlos as teammates. While playing for Real Madrid against Manchester United, Ronaldo produced one of his greatest performances. He scored an amazing hattrick that helped to knock United out of the 2002–03 Champions League. The United home fans joined the Real Madrid fans to give Ronaldo a standing ovation when he was substituted.

The most unfortunate thing about Ronaldo is how good he might have been if he had remained injury free, partied less, and was determined to get the very best from himself (he was well known for not training as hard as others, especially in the latter part of his career). He might have become the indisputably greatest of all time.

Ronaldo's struggles can teach us many things. It can motivate us to not leave our success in football or life to be open to the question: what might have been? The most valuable lesson, though, is that resolute desire, patience and hard work can triumph even in the most unlikely circumstances. It was Ronaldo's love for the game and desire to play again that ultimately enabled him to return triumphantly. Despite the repeated bursts of pain from each injury, surgeries, rehabilitation, heartbreak due to failed attempts to return, and loss of time, Ronaldo's desire and his self-belief led to one of the most glorious comebacks in sport.

Ronaldo's comeback in the World Cup is connected to one of my own personal success stories. I had smoked marijuana from about the age of ten and I was addicted soon after I started. I tried to stop many times. One time I was smoking marijuana and had eaten too much of an extremely potent dope cake (a cake made with marijuana). The mother of all lightning storms exploded in my mind, which scared the hell out of me. I was thirteen years old. I cried and asked my Mum to help me. I was taken to hospital and fed a large amount of liquid charcoal. Later, I was told that I had nearly died.

Just before the 2002 World Cup commenced, I made a deal with myself. If Ronaldo scored in every game, scored more goals than had been scored by the leading scorer in the past six tournaments (more than six), scored a hattrick in the final and won the World Cup, I would stop smoking marijuana, for good. I was very disappointed that Ronaldo didn't score against England, but I was annoyingly loud (according to my mother) when Ronaldo scored a fantastic goal against Turkey in the semi-final.

Just before the final I smoked what I told myself would be my last hit and said that even though Ronaldo hadn't scored against England and he had only scored six goals so far, if Brazil win and he gets a hattrick, that will be my last one. Witnessing Ronaldo score the two goals in the final, his numerous chances, his overall performance and the joy on his face when he realised he had won the World Cup brought tears to my eyes. That was enough for me. I have not smoked marijuana since and I never will again.

This experience taught me that external sources of inspiration can strengthen one's own desire to overcome adversity. My desire to *stop* smoking marijuana had not been strong enough to conquer my desire *to* smoke marijuana. But, my joy caused by witnessing Ronaldo's resurrection produced a firm state in my mind and this motivated me to avoid any situations that involved smoking marijuana. Sometimes our desire is not strong enough to surmount a persistent obstacle, but the power of our desire can be increasingly strengthened by external sources of assistance, resulting in overwhelming motivational power.

Your triumphs need not be witnessed by other people for them to be worthwhile and meaningful. Conquering addiction, overcoming your fears, and self-improvement of any kind demand a great deal from the human spirit. Unfortunately, most people succumb to their bad habits and give up on realising the beautiful vision they have of themselves and the life they would like to live. Still, within you is the power to overcome adversity and achieve your goals, and it is up to you to unleash it.

The cause of the triumph of the human spirit is the same, whether it be in private or public. Unshakable determination can overcome almost any obstacle that confronts us.

CONCLUSION

I HAVE PRESENTED my reflections on the game of football and the game of life. My aim was to discover insights into these games we play and the principles that underlie them. Incorporation of these insights and principles into our decision-making can elevate our performances in football and other areas of life.

Nonetheless, this book is really about the value of thinking. Reflection on football and life can give rise to new ideas that enable us to perceive the world afresh. As the wisest teach us, a thinking life, which involves the pursuit and application of wisdom, is essential to living a good life. This book has highlighted the value of ideas for mastering football and life.

This book is also an invitation to think deeply about the issues and things that matter to you. Reading books like this one, proverbs and wise quotes can trigger this kind of thinking in you, which can lead to your own discovery of principles you can use to understand life and to do better in it. The more you think about football or life, the better you will understand them and the more effective your actions in those games will be.

We should study the masters in football and life. Their wisdom was earned by overcoming the obstacles that confronted them. We can save ourselves time and struggle and avoid repeating the same mistakes by applying their wisdom to our own lives. Many times the wise thought of a master has erased a worrying thought in my own mind or helped me with some personal difficulty.

The idea that thinking or philosophy is necessary to be able to flourish in the games of football or life is absurd to many people. In addition, many philosophers complain that ordinary people are not interested in ideas. In my experience, this complaint is justified. Not only non-philosophers, but also professional philosophers have said to me philosophy has little practical value or it is 'intellectual masturbation'. I urge you to reject this attitude to philosophy.

Once you get into the habit of reflecting on football or life, you are likely to find that your thirst for wisdom and good ideas will continually grow. You will come to understand that the power of thought pervades human existence. A human mind that denies the value of ideas and thinking is like a fish that denies the value and existence of the water in which it swims. All of us are always swimming in an ocean of ideas.

The word 'philosophy' originated from the Greek language and consists of two words, *philo* and *sophia*. *Philo* means 'loving' and *sophia* means 'wisdom'. Evidently, this book is a gateway to philosophy, the love of wisdom. I encourage you to seek out the greatest philosophers in history, as well as scientists and other great thinkers in every domain of thought, wisdom and knowledge, including from the great ethical and religious traditions.

Thinking and ideas are catalysts for change. Emerson wrote, 'Beware when the great God lets loose a thinker on this planet. Then all things are at risk.' All human-made things will be at risk because these things are based on ideas. A thinker or philosopher questions the ideas of the status quo, and if the ideas are found wanting, their change or substitution will be demanded. Change is something people generally don't like, especially those who are invested in the ideas or things dependent on them.

Here is another observation, also made by Emerson: 'What is the hardest task in the world? To think.' Sometimes we will find the activity of thinking strenuous and so we will be tempted to do something less so. Do not give up too soon, for all human values depend on ideas. Justice, love, law, money, football and virtually all human thoughts are ideas. These ideas consist of other ideas and many of them are attached to powerful emotions, symbols, objects or activities. Our ideas determine what we think and do, so ideas are crucial to what we do and our results in life. Thinking is a safeguard to protect us against bad or false ideas. Therefore, thinking and good ideas are essential to achieving mastery in the game of football and the game of life.